The Psychology of Jesus

Practical Help for
Living in Relationship

Third Edition

By David W. Jones

Front Cover: *Return of The Prodigal Son*
by Bartolome Esteban Murillo

Back Cover:
The Return of the Prodigal Son
by James Tissot
The Return of the Prodigal
Rembrandt Harmenszoon van Rijn
Sacred Heart
Odion Redon

Contents

Introduction to Revised 2014 Edition

Since the initial writing of *The Psychology of Jesus*, I've used it in small group discussions, with people in counseling, and have shared it with college and seminary professors across the United States. In response to these interactions, I've reedited the book for this new edition keeping the lesson of this story in mind...

A man went to see his counselor. "Here's my problem," he said. "Every night, I am so afraid there are monsters under my bed that I can't sleep. I know they aren't real, but no matter how much I tell myself they are not there, it doesn't help. I even tried sleeping under my bed, but then I was so convinced there were monsters on top, I still couldn't sleep. What can I do?"

"I think I can help you," said the counselor. "Let's start with two sessions per week at $150/hour. In about six months, you should see a noticeable difference."

"Will I be able to sleep?" he asked.

"Only time can tell," replied the counselor.

"I have no other choice," the man said, "sign me up."

The man came regularly for three months but then missed the next three sessions. The counselor called, "Is there something wrong? Aren't you going to continue in your therapy?"

"I was," the man said, "but now I'm sleeping fine."

"What made the difference?" the counselor asked.

"Well, after I talked to you, I called my minister. He came over and cut the legs off my bed."

In this edition, I've tried to trim out the excess to make this a more readable and helpful book for individuals, couples, and classes. My hope is that this version will offer even more practical tools to aid in your sleeping, your waking, and in all your relating.

David W. Jones
January 1, 2014

Introduction

"That your family?" the man across from me on the Marta train in Atlanta asked.

"Yes," I replied. I had watched him talk to the woman behind him as if they were old friends, and now, he turned toward me.

"They're beautiful."

"Thanks," I said.

"What's your name?" he asked.

"David," I said. "What's yours?"

"Jim," he replied. He leaned across the aisle. I met him in the middle. We shook hands. His breath told me there would be three in this conversation: Jim, me, and whatever he'd been drinking before he got on the train.

"What's your name?" he asked again.

"David," I said again.

"What do you do?" he asked.

"I'm a minister," I replied.

"Oh, hell no," he said.

"Oh, hell yes," I said.

The people around us laughed, surprised at my choice of words, but my words made sense to me. If I was going to talk to Jim, I would say and hear more by beginning with his speech, not mine. The language we choose when trying to communicate with others is important. In this book, in an unusual combination, I am going to use the language of psychology and exegesis (what professional Christians call Bible study). It is as atypical for a pastor to talk about Freud, Adler, Frankl or Glasser as it is for a psychologist or a professor of psychology to talk about Peter, Mary, Martha or Pilate. Psychologists, seeing themselves as scientists, tend to avoid people of the Bible, and preachers, seeing themselves as advocates of faith, typically disregard the concepts and language of psychology.

This linguistic specialization is unfortunate because the language of psychology illuminates the men and women in the Bible, and they, in turn, offer lucid illustrations of psychological principles.

Before we begin, we must have a clear definition of *psychology*. The accepted definition is *the study of mental processes, how the*

7

mind works, how we think (2008). This definition is limited because psychology looks at far more than just the intellect. So, for our approach, I add an older definition of *psychology* as *study of the soul (1653).[i]* The root here is the Greek *psyche* which means, *soul, spirit,* and *breath. Breath* has a long tradition of being synonymous with spirit or life. For example, in the Genesis 2 account of creation God breathes life into the human.

The purpose of the book is to offer practical help for living in relationship from the field of psychology and from the gospel accounts of the life of Jesus. Each chapter offers a primary concept from psychology, an encounter with Jesus from one of the gospels, a deeper examination of the concept using the gospel text, a practical application, and then a space for personal reflection. As a pastor, I am not an expert in psychology. With any of the theories mentioned, I encourage you to study further those that interest you. In no way should this book replace your own thinking, your own examination of scripture, psychology, or life, but instead encourage you to think, read, examine, apply, integrate, relate, and grow.

Now I invite you to journey with me in the pages ahead, to examine the mental processes in the gospels and your own mental processes, to examine the souls in scripture and your own soul, and hopefully, to find your story in scripture and scripture in your story.

Are you ready? Then let's begin.

Head of Christ
Rembrandt

Who is this Jesus?
Why is he different?
– Pilate
Jesus Christ Superstar

Chapter One: Mary Magdalene

Primary Concept:
"Who am I?" and "What's wrong with me?"
are not helpful questions.

Who are you?
Go ahead. Think about it. Let's answer it together.

First, what titles do you have? Mr., Mrs., Miss...
I am a Reverend. (I have tried to get my congregations to call me the Right Reverend or Most High Pastor, but so far they have refused. Most drop all titles and just call me David.)

What roles do you play? Include family roles and professional roles.
I am a son, brother, husband, father, pastor, preacher, teacher, sometimes-coach, volunteer...

Who is the most famous person you have ever met?
When I was twelve, I met Valerie Bertinelli from the television series *One Day at a Time*. She, then sixteen, told me I was cute.

What are your achievements?
I've been married for twenty-five years. I have pastored in three churches. I've authored seven books. I have a couple of master's degrees.

What are your failures?
I keep a list in my mind of every job in my life I didn't get. I have a wall of books that I started but never finished. I've preached quite a few flat sermons. I remember a few girls from high school that wouldn't go out with me. I remember in middle school when I set the record for the slowest time to run a mile. My list has some obscure and silly shames that I've yet to let go of. For example, I once asked an in-law if she was pregnant when she wasn't, and I bought a Milli Vanilli album even after I learned they lip synced it. My list goes on and on.

What adjectives would you use to describe yourself?

I came up with a dualistic list: saint/sinner, organized/messy, faithful/ fearful, workaholic/lazy, patient/hurried...

How much time have you spent in your life trying to answer "Who am I?"

Much of my life has been a quest to answer this foundational question, "Who am I?" My search has taken me many places, to school, to work, to church. I looked for answers from parents, teachers, friends, acquaintances, strangers, libraries, the media, and God. I looked in what I own, what I do, what I think about myself, and what others say about me. The struggle to answer "Who am I?" has shaped my behavior and my relationships.

Psychology, as a field, has been centered on helping us in this search to answer, "Who am I?" Most people, when you mention psychology, think first of Sigmund Freud. Freud is still considered the father of modern psychology and he offered some of the widest known answers to "Who am I?" Freud, like many others in the field, focused on a variation to our "Who am I?" question. Because people came to Freud with problems, Freud wanted to help them answer the question they asked him, "What's wrong with me?"

As Freud studied and theorized about humanity, he had one main assertion. Freud concluded from his observations that, as humans, we have lots of things wrong with us. He said, *I have found little that is "good" about human beings on the whole. In my experience most of them are trash, no matter whether they publicly subscribe to this or that ethical doctrine or to none at all.* According to Freud, we are trashed by nature which has given us drives we can't satisfy, and personalities (split into the id, ego, and superego) which we can't calm. According to Freud, we are also trashed by our   nurture, usually our mothers, which potty trained us too soon or breast fed us too long.

Though the diagnoses have changed, the Freudian approach to problems is still popular. "Having a difficulty? The difficulty is you." The diagnosis you hear may be, "You are obsessive compulsive; or you are bipolar; or you are chronically depressed; or you are hypersynomic; or you are schizophrenic." Or the diagnosis may tell you that you have a disorder; "You have Delusional Disorder; or you have Dependent Personality Disorder; or you have Depressive Disorder; or you have Disruptive Behavior Disorder," (and those are just the 'D's). The typical therapeutic cycle is: counsel, diagnose, treat (often medicate), and repeat.

Psychology has had no monopoly on diagnosing psyche or souls – the church was distributing diagnoses long before the science of psychology. Freud calling human beings "trash on the whole" is surprising when you discover he was Jewish because he sounds like a good Calvinist. John Calvin (1536) used the words *total depravity* in talking about human nature. The Westminster Confession (1646) in the Calvinist tradition, said that human nature is *utterly indisposed, disabled, and made opposite to all good, and wholly inclined to all evil,* and from it *do proceed all actual transgressions.*

Psychology in the Freudian tradition and Christianity in the tradition of Calvin have diagnosed the condition of humanity and said, "There is something really wrong with us."

The assertion of this chapter, this book, and many voices in psychology lesser known than Freud and in Christianity lesser known than Calvin, is not that Freud or Calvin, the psychologist or the preacher, came up with wrong, incorrect or defective answers. We may be 'trash' or 'totally depraved'. The assertion is not that the diagnoses offered by professionals today aren't accurate. They may be. The assertion is that all these diagnoses of mind and soul have not been and are not now especially helpful. The reason is simple. The answers these diagnoses offer come from a primary question of "Who am I?" which offers us little assistance in living life.

From the psychologist, we may hear that we are defective or disordered, but their diagnosis hasn't made us any less dysfunctional. From the preacher we may hear that we are depraved sinners, but their proclamation hasn't made us sin any less. The answers from psychologist and pastor alike may be accurate – it's just that their foundational questions: "Who am I?" and "What's wrong with me?" are not especially helpful. For two thousand years of Christianity and over two hundred years of psychology, so much energy has been spent asking the wrong questions.

Fortunately for us, these questions of, "Who am I?" and "What's wrong with me?" weren't ongoing unanswerable questions for Jesus and his psychology.

Text

Before we go onto the more significant questions in Jesus' psychology, I want us to examine just how futile "Who am I?" and "What's wrong with me?" are for us and were for the followers of Jesus. The best example of their futility is found at the end of the gospels. I assume that the story of Jesus is not like a murder mystery and that I don't need to offer a spoiler alert since you already know how it ends. So, beginning at the end, let's look at Jesus' followers, right before Easter in John chapter 20.

As you read this passage, imagine you are Mary Magdalene coming to the grave site, imagine you are John and Peter racing toward the tomb, and that you are the rest of the disciples hiding. You may want to read the verses a few times and imagine yourself as a different character each time.

As you read the passage, try and answer "Who am I?" as you think the character would.

John 20: *Early on the first day of the week, while it was still dark, Mary Magdalene came to the tomb and saw that the stone had been removed from the tomb. 2 So she ran and went to Simon Peter and the other disciple, the one whom Jesus loved, and said to them, "They have taken the Lord out of the tomb, and we do not know where they have laid him."*

3 Then Peter and the other disciple set out and went toward the tomb. 4 The two were running together, but the other disciple outran Peter and reached the tomb first. 5 He bent down to look in and saw the linen wrappings lying there, but he did not go in. 6 Then Simon Peter came, following him, and went into the tomb. He saw the linen wrappings lying there, 7 and the cloth that had been on Jesus' head, not lying with the linen wrappings but rolled up in a place by itself. 8 Then the other disciple, who reached the tomb first, also went in, and he saw and believed; 9 for as yet they did not understand the scripture, that he must rise from the dead. 10 Then the disciples returned to their homes. 11 But Mary stood weeping outside the tomb. As she wept, she bent over to look into the tomb; 12 and she saw two angels in white, sitting where the body of Jesus had been lying, one at the head and the other at the feet.

13 They said to her, "Woman, why are you weeping?" She said to them, "They have taken away my Lord, and I do not know where they have laid him." 14 When she had said this, she turned around and saw Jesus standing there, but she did not know that it was Jesus.

15 Jesus said to her, "Woman, why are you weeping? Whom are you looking for?"

Supposing him to be the gardener, she said to him, "Sir, if you have carried him away, tell me where you have laid him, and I will take him away."

16 Jesus said to her, "Mary!"

She turned and said to him in Hebrew, "Rabbouni!" (which means Teacher).

17 Jesus said to her, "Do not hold on to me, because I have not yet ascended to the Father. But go to my brothers and say to them, 'I am ascending to my Father and your Father, to my God and your God.'"

18 Mary Magdalene went and announced to the disciples, "I have seen the Lord"; and she told them that he had said these things to her.

Concept in the text

What did you think about as you imagined yourself as Mary? Peter? John? the other disciples? How did you feel? How would each answer "Who am I?" before going to the tomb on Easter morning.

For Mary Magdalene, Jesus was Rabbi, teacher, friend, leader and companion. Yet, just two days prior to this passage she had watched him die a painful death of torture on the cross. Soldiers had separated her from Jesus. While he died, she couldn't get to him or give him any relief. She would have saved him if she could, but she couldn't. All she could do was watch, pray, cry.

On the day of this passage, on Easter morning, she was on her way to the tomb. She was concerned about the rock which covered the entrance. She didn't know how she would move it. It might be an immovable separation for her. She was also worried about soldiers. They kept her from Jesus on the cross. She was worried guards might be at the tomb and keep her from Jesus' body.

If she would have been asked on her way to the tomb, "Mary, who are you?" She would have likely used words like, "Weak. Powerless. Heartbroken. I wanted to save him but I couldn't. I wanted to help him but I couldn't."

While Mary watched Jesus die, the disciples had been hiding. They didn't see Jesus die. They hadn't been near him. They hadn't stood up for him. They had let him die without them. They had done nothing to try and save him. On the morning of the passage, Easter morning, if you were to ask them, "Who are you?" They would have likely said, "We are failures. We should have been with Jesus, but we ran. We were and are afraid. We hid and are hiding. They came for Jesus and took him. They will probably come for us. We are weak. We are powerless. We couldn't stop them from taking Jesus. We won't be able to keep them from taking us."

Finally, besides Mary Magdalene and the disciples, what about Jesus? What about Jesus on Easter morning before sunrise? How would he have answered, "Who am I?" The answer is...he wouldn't. Here's where the "Who am I?" question falls apart. Jesus couldn't have answered it, as far as we can tell, before sunrise. The answer for Jesus wasn't many words like Mary or the disciples. The answer for Jesus was one word, a single word others would have to give for him. The word was 'dead.' "Who is Jesus?" someone might ask. "Jesus is dead," was the answer.

Concept in Depth

The problem with "Who am I?" as an approach to the human mind, the human soul, is that our answers turn out like the people's in the text. Sooner or later we fail, we fall short. Sooner or later, there is some rock too big to move, some past too dark to erase. Even if we never experience those dark moments that question character and ability, sooner or later we will fail at the primary evolutionary task, surviving. We are wired with this internal goal – stay alive, don't die. All existing creatures want to keep on existing, but eventually we all fail. The wealthy the poor, the hero and the villain, we all die. Then, no matter how we have answered "Who am I?" with our titles, our roles, our adjectives, successes or failures, satisfactions or disappointments, sooner or later we won't be able to answer "Who

16

am I?" for ourselves. All answers will have to be given for us. Friends and others may eulogize us well. "He was a good man." "She was a nice person." "He was wealthy." "She was powerful." No matter how high the praise, all answers will be past tense – and past tense only. The only present tense answer allowed is, "She is dead." "He is dead." That was all anyone could say for Jesus. That's all anyone will be able to say for us.

So, "Who am I?" is a fleeting, cursory, superficial, short-lived, passing, perfunctory, temporal, transitory, and all in all deficient question because none of our answers last.

Fortunately, Jesus offers a different approach. Unlike our exercise at the beginning of the chapter, Jesus did not answer "Who am I?" with a title. People tried to call him "Messiah" all through the gospel of Mark, and Jesus told them to keep quiet. He did not answer with a position or role. He didn't define himself by achievements or failures. He had no résumé. He was not impressed with others attempts at self-definition, no titles or achievements stirred him. No record of failures brought to him by others made an impact. Jesus was secure in his understanding of himself and of others. From this confidence, he went forward into other questions. In the next chapter, we'll examine how Jesus answered, "Who am I?" for himself and in the rest of the book we'll look at the more helpful questions in Jesus' psychology.

Application

Before we move onward, let's look backward. Who are the significant people in your life that have shaped how you answer, "Who am I?" More than accurate definitions of who we are, labels often give us the roles we live into.

Adele Faber, author of *How to Talk so Kids Will Listen and Listen so Kids Will Talk,* tells of the birth of her son. She and her husband chose to name him, "David", which means, "Beloved". He also picked up another label.

I remember the moment when my son, David, as born. Five seconds had gone by and he still hadn't breathed. I was terrified. The nurse slapped him on his back. No response. The tension was excruciating. She said, "He's a stubborn one!" Still no response. A moment later he finally cried – that piercing sound of the newborn. My relief was indescribable. But later on that day, I found myself wondering. "Is he really stubborn?" By the time I brought him home from the hospital, I had put the nurse's comment in place – foolish words from a foolish woman Imagine putting a label on an infant less that half a minute old!

And yet every time during the next few years, when he kept on crying no matter how long I patted or rocked him, when he wouldn't try a new food, when he refused to take his nap, when he balked at getting on the bus to nursery school, when he wouldn't wear a sweater on a cold day, the thought would flit through my mind, "She was right. He is stubborn."[ii]

Labels can be as lasting as names, both we receive often from well-meaning adults and friends who are working, they believe, in our best interest even if in harmful ways like the following story shared by Mike Yacconelli. As you read it, remind yourself, the teacher all along believes that she is being helpful to her student.

At the end of recess, Margaret was still outside. When she realized that she was late, she ran but her hurrying was to no avail. The class had returned to their desks and their teacher was waiting for her.

"Margaret!" she yelled in disgust. "We've been waiting for you! Come up to the front of the class right now."

The teacher then addressed the class, "Friends, Margaret has been bad. I've tried to help her to do better and to be better, but she refuses to learn. We will all help her see how much her self-centeredness has hurt the class. We will all be her teachers. I want each of you to come to the front of the room and write on the blackboard something bad about Margaret. Hopefully this experience will help her learn to be a better person, to be a good girl and not a bad girl like she's been."[iii]

You can imagine some of the things they wrote. Margaret remembered them for years. This story may seem overly violent. If you are so many years from school, especially middle school, ask a young teen if she or he can identify with Margaret. Find a school teacher and ask if the story sounds familiar.

The main point of sharing with you Margaret's story is this – Margaret's teacher and her class thought they were helping her. They were trying to help Margaret by telling her she was *fat, stupid,* and *lazy.* We approach friend and family often with a diagnosing label in mind trying to be helpful, "Let me help you see what's wrong with you."

Challenge for Us

In the psychology of Jesus, Jesus doesn't spend a lot of time on the questions, "Who am I?" and "What's wrong with me?" or "Who are you?" and "What's wrong with you?" The challenge for us is to see where the diagnosis of self and others has led to pain, and then search for a better, healthier, more productive approach.

Reflection

Read the following quotes. How do they relate to the psychology of Jesus and the first encounter with Jesus mentioned above.

In a very real sense not one of us is qualified, but it seems that God continually chooses the most unqualified to do his work, to bear his glory. If we are qualified, we tend to think that we have done the job ourselves. If we are forced to accept our evident lack of qualification, then there's no danger that we will confuse God's work with our own, or God's glory with our own. Madeleine L'Engle

The greatest happiness of life is the conviction that we are loved -- loved for ourselves, or rather, loved in spite of ourselves. Victor Hugo

Self-rejection is the greatest enemy of the spiritual life because it contradicts the sacred voice that calls us the Beloved. Being the Beloved expresses the core truth of our existence. Henri Nouwen

Exercise:

Make a list of people who have given you different labels or diagnoses in your life.

Beside each person's name, write the label you heard from them.

Beside the label write 'help,' 'hinder,' or 'both' as you determine whether the diagnosis has been a help, hindrance, or both to your personal growth.

Now, go back through your list. Put an X through any labels you wish to leave behind and circle those labels you wish to carry forward.

Now repeat the exercise with labels not from others but labels you give yourself.

Seated Christ
Vasily Polenov 1887

One does not become fully human painlessly.
Rollo May

Chapter Two: God

Primary Concept:
We can't answer "Who am I?" for ourselves.
Someone else must do it for us.

I am the father of three children: Cayla, Abbie, and Nathan. One day, I overheard Abbie (then 5) and Nathan (3) playing together. Abbie declared, "We're going to play grocery store." They often role played games together with Abbie directing, writing, starring, and usually telling Nathan what to do and say. "I'll be the clerk," she said. "This will be my counter." Abbie paused for a moment and said to Nathan, "And who are you going to be?"

"I don't know," Nathan responded, "you haven't told me yet."

In life, like Nathan, we often look to others to tell us who we are.

"Who am I?" is a difficult question for everyone because we cannot answer it on our own. We can only answer "Who am I?" in relationship. Like Nathan, we look to others to tell us what value we offer, what purpose we have, and what roles we play as they answer, "Who am I?" for us. Sociologist/ Psychologist Charles Horton Cooley called our understanding of self which we shape from the input of others as our *looking glass self*. Cooley said, *Each to each a looking-glass, Reflects the other that doth pass.*

Like the rest of us, Jesus did not answer "Who am I?" on his own. He did not try. He looked to another. The passage below is the first public appearance of Jesus as he begins his ministry starting with his baptism by John the Baptizer in the Jordan River. After Jesus is baptized, he hears a voice from heaven that tells him who he is. Read the following passage. Imagine you are Jesus. What does the voice from heaven sound like? How do you feel when you hear it?

Text

Matthew 3: *13 Then Jesus came from Galilee to John at the Jordan, to be baptized by him. 14 John would have prevented him, saying, "I need to be baptized by you, and do you come to me?"*

15 But Jesus answered him, "Let it be so now; for it is proper for us in this way to fulfill all righteousness." Then he consented.

16 And when Jesus had been baptized, just as he came up from the water, suddenly the heavens were opened to him and he saw the Spirit of God descending like a dove and alighting on him.

17 And a voice from heaven said, "This is my Son, the Beloved, with whom I am well pleased."

4: Then Jesus was led up by the Spirit into the wilderness to be tempted by the devil. 2 He fasted forty days and forty nights, and afterwards he was famished.

3 The tempter came and said to him, "If you are the Son of God...

Concept in the Text

Jesus doesn't spend much time on the question, "Who am I?" because for him, it wasn't a lifelong riddle which he needed to go from person to person or institution to institution for information about his identity. He had a primary source. He found his answer in the voice of God. Certainly there were times in his life when his sense of value, of self-worth, of being beloved by God, was questioned. There were times when his identity as he understood it was challenged. But, for the most part, Jesus was not one who needed to go out and find himself, not one who needed to prove who he was at another's expense, not one with a chip on his shoulder seeking response, or one who needed a crowd to affirm his personal worth. Jesus understood himself to be loved, and, for him, that was enough.

Concept in Depth

Jesus' sense of self-worth was defined by love, but the word *love* is used in so many ways. I say, "I love ice cream. I love college basketball. I love a rainy night..." and I also say, "I love my wife. I love my children. I love God..." To say, "I love ice cream, my children, and God," all in the same sentence or paragraph implies that those loves are the same or at least similar. They are not. Same four letters, same word, but different implications.

Before I can advance the theme of this book, I must address this problem of the word *love* and the questions *love* brings. For example, how did Jesus understand love? Was Jesus thinking of my love for my wife, when he said, "Love thy neighbor?" Was Jesus thinking of my love of ice cream when he said, "Love the Lord your God with all your heart, soul, mind and strength?" How did Jesus understand himself as loved by God? What do we mean when we say that God loved Jesus? When we say that God loves humanity or that God loves us or that God so loved the world? What do we mean in these contexts when we say, *Love.*

Some languages have it easier. The Greeks have more than one word for love. They have *eros, philio, agape.* Those choices seem to have suited them well. Yet, to write in English, I haven't found a lot of help in substituting Greek or any other unfamiliar words. To explore love in the mind of Jesus, in the psychology of Jesus and how he loved rather than new words for 'love,' I propose in Jesus that we see love in two forms, two types, two kinds which are both familiar and universal.

Both types of love are full of wonder, joy, and excitement. Both forms can be puzzling, overwhelming and painful. Both kinds give life meaning and can make any day worth living. Yet, one, more than the other, can be found in God as described in the gospels and understood by Jesus. One, more than the other, is what shaped Jesus understanding of himself, served as the foundation for what he taught, and defined the norms with which he treated others. One, more than the other, is found at the center of the psychology of Jesus.[iv]

Love type #1: Value Recognizing Love

Value recognizing love is a beautiful type of love. When we 'fall in love,' we are experiencing value recognizing love. This love marks, observes, notes, appreciates, and celebrates value. As the saying goes, "Beauty is in the eyes of the beholder." This love appreciates the beauty it beholds as worthwhile and valuable. To someone you love, you may say, "You are so beautiful." "You are so strong." "You are so smart." In doing so, we show our appreciation for the person's beauty, strength, and intelligence. We say words that all of us want to hear, "I find value in you! I love you because of who you are." Value recognizing love can lift the spirits, give connection, foster joy and happiness, and affirm identity. For this love, value = good feelings.

Sports Fans show value recognizing love. When a football team wins, people show up at the airport to welcome them home. "You are so amazing! You're the greatest! We love you! Yeah!" Winning feels great for players and fans alike. However, when the football team loses, and loses repeatedly, the fans don't come. They don't see value. No one shows up at the airport and says, "You are so average! You are actually less than par! We love you!" When you lose, there is no love because there is no achievement therefore no value to be appreciated. No value = no feelings or bad feelings.

While value recognizing love can be a very wonderful sort of love, it can also be a very painful sort of love. In marriages, or in any longer term relationships, there can come a time when value recognizing love no longer perceives any value. Those who once proclaimed appreciation, approval and admiration, become quiet – or worse as they become negative. "You used to be so... this and that... now you are just ...neither this nor that. You're not the same person I fell in love with. You changed. You're different." This essentially means, "I saw value. Now I see none." Or, perhaps even more painfully, "I don't know why I loved you in the first place."

Sooner or later, lives built on value recognizing love alone, bring us pain. In our insecurity, we go from person to person, relationship to relationship, asking, "Do you find any value in me? Do you like me?" terrified that our significant others, our mirrors for forming our sense of self-worth don't see value, and we ache. Elizabeth KublerRoss summed up life under value recognizing love when she wrote, *Most of us have been raised as prostitutes. I will love you "if." And this word "if" has ruined or destroyed more lives than anything else on this planet earth. It prostitutes us; it makes us feel that we can buy love with good behavior, or good grades... If we were not able to accommodate the grown-ups, we were punished...*[v]

Fortunately, there is another type of love.

Love Type #2: Value Giving Love

Value giving love doesn't recognize value, but it gives value. It doesn't require, but it offers. It doesn't demand, but it empowers. Value giving love is the type of love Jesus trusted in and offered to others.

To understand this love, we must do more than study the life of

Jesus, we must do more than ponder the teachings of Jesus, we must do more than believe in Jesus. To understand this love, the best exercise is for us to imagine ourselves as Jesus. For many of us, imagining ourselves as Jesus is not an easy task as Scott Peck related,

Not long ago I participated in a conference of Christian therapists and counselors, where the speaker, Harvey Cox, a Baptist theologian, told the Gospel story of Jesus being called to resuscitate the daughter of a wealthy Roman. As Jesus is going to the Roman's house, a woman who has been hemorrhaging for years reaches out from the crowd and touches His robe. He feels her touch and turns around and asks, "Who touched me?" The woman comes forward and begs Him to cure her and He does, and then goes on to the house of the Roman whose daughter had died.

After telling the story, Cox asked this audience of six hundred mostly Christian professionals whom they identified with. When he asked who identified with the bleeding woman, about a hundred raised their hands. When he asked who identified with the anxious Roman father, more of the rest raised their hands. When he asked who identified with the curious crowd, most raised their hands. But when he asked who identified with Jesus, only six people raised their hands.

Something is very wrong here. Of six hundred more or less professional Christians, only one out of a hundred identified with Jesus. Maybe more actually did but were afraid to raise their hands lest that seem arrogant. But again something is wrong with our concept of Christianity if it seems arrogant to identify with Jesus. That is exactly what we are supposed to do! We're supposed to identify with Jesus, act like Jesus, be like Jesus. That is what Christianity is supposed to be about the imitation of Christ.[vi]

In numerous places throughout the book, I will ask you as I have already to imagine you are a character from the gospel text. These exercises are crucial to understand the Psychology of Jesus, especially in this chapter. Jesus lived his life, saw others, was able to love, risk, try, grow, reach, do all because he lived under this second type of love. To understand this value giving love, we must put ourselves into the story of Jesus. To understand the psychology of Jesus, how he thought of himself and how he approached others, we must imagine ourselves as Jesus. We must be Jesus.

Jesus' baptism is the doorway to answering how a foundational answer to "Who am I?" can shape our lives. So, before we can go any further, imagine you are Jesus on the day of your baptism. Let me give you some background. Some of this I am speculating, but most comes from what we know of Jesus from the gospels.

You are walking with the crowd toward the Jordan River.

You know this is the first step for you in beginning what you believe God is calling you to do.

You have waited for a long time for this. As the oldest child in the family, you stayed home to help raise your brothers and sisters. You worked as a carpenter, helping the family by making what money you could. Now that your siblings are old enough to take care of themselves, you start to follow the calling you received from your heavenly father. This begins at the Jordan River.

What others think of you is in the air. Some have heard John speak of you, though he didn't mention your name. There are whisperings in the crowd. You hear them as you move forward, but there is another voice you long to hear.

You walk to the water. John says he should be baptized by you, you tell him this is part of a greater purpose. You know you are there for another voice. Another voice you had heard before.

You go under the water as John pushes down. You rise up. You feel the Spirit of God descend like a dove. A voice speaks, "You are my child. Beloved."

Yes. That was the voice you were listening for...

In Jesus we find good news for all about God's type of love. Jesus heard the voice of God not at the end of his ministry, but at the beginning, before he healed anyone, before he taught anyone, before he did – anything! He didn't do great things so that he would be loved. Jesus did great things because he understood he was loved. The love which declared his value gave him the freedom to grow, to question, to reach, to think, to feel, to believe, to care, and most of all, to love. If we see ourselves as Jesus, then we will understand the baptism story of Jesus in scripture belongs not just to Jesus, but to all of us as God says to us for the entire world to hear, "You are my child, my beloved." If we see ourselves as Jesus, then we can claim God's declaration of Jesus as the declaration of us, we are God's children, beloved. If we can see ourselves as Jesus, we understand that "beloved" is a label that comes from God, is as set in stone as the Ten Commandments, and is beyond human threat, challenge or question. If we can see ourselves as Jesus, then we can let go of "Who am I?" as a question answered, a mystery solved, a riddle explained, and liberated, we can move, like Jesus, onto other questions. If we can see ourselves as Jesus, we can not only claim value for ourselves, but offer it to others, letting others know they have value, they are beloved.

Application

For those living under value recognizing love, a simple voice of value giving love can be life changing.

Fred Craddock is a famous preacher and teacher of preaching. He and his wife were vacationing in Gatlinburg, Tennessee. They were enjoying breakfast together, when an elderly man came over to the table. The man obviously had a story to tell, and he didn't know the Craddocks so he sighted them as a fresh audience.

The man spoke, "Hey, my name is Ben Hooper, what is yours?"

"Mine is Fred Craddock."

Then the older gentleman said, "What do you do?"

Craddock sighed, his goal of some alone time with his wife was clearly threatened. He replied, "I am a professor of homiletics at a seminary," hoping the lofty title would scare the intruder away.

Then the man said, "Oh, you're a preacher." He then pulled up a chair and sat down. "I've got a preacher story for you. Mind if I join you?"

Fred said nothing. Ben Hooper began his tale, "I grew up in those hills over there. I was what they called an illegitimate child. They called me names everywhere I went. When I went to school I always sat in the back of the room because I was ashamed of who I was. When I walked down the street, I had this terrible feeling that everyone was looking at me and saying, 'I wonder who his father is?' My mother would never tell me who my father was. I never knew. I was so ashamed.

"When I was thirteen years old, a preacher came to town one day and everybody was talking about how good he was. I wanted to see this new preacher. I snuck in after the service had started so no one would see me. Then I snuck out before it was over so that no one would speak to me. I have to admit that he was a good preacher. I went back the next Sunday and the next Sunday always sneaking out so that no one could speak to me. One Sunday though, the sermon was so good that I forgot to leave. And before I knew what was happening they had sung the last hymn and everyone was pushing out into the aisle. I tried to get out of the church, but before I could make my way through the crowd, I felt a hand on my shoulder. I turned and I looked. It was the preacher. He was 6'4" and dressed in black. He looked down at me and he said, "Hey, son. What's your name? Whose boy are you? Who's your father? Whose son are you?"

Then Ben said, "Mr., when he asked me whose son I was, I almost started to cry. I felt so hurt. Then he suddenly said, "I know who you are. I know who your father is. There is such a close family resemblance I couldn't have missed it no matter how hard I tried." I looked up into that preacher's face because I felt that maybe he knew who I was. Maybe he held the secret to my identity. And he looked down at me and said, "I know who you are. You look just like your father." Then he said to me, "You are a child of God."

Then Ben said, "Mr., that simple statement changed my life. And that's my preacher story," then he got up and he left.

The waitress came over and asked the Craddocks, "Do you know who that was?"

"Ben Hooper?" Fred asked.

"That's right," she replied, "Ben Hooper, former governor of Tennessee."

Ben Hooper had lived in the shame that is the byproduct of a psychology built on value recognizing love. Because his family history was different than others, because he had no male parent that saw value in him, he could see no value in himself. The hand of the minister and his declaration came like a voice of God to Ben. He went forward from that day living in a world shaped not by value recognizing love, but value giving love. He went forward able to do great things not in hopes of seeing himself as loved but because he believed that he was loved.

Challenge for Us

Jesus didn't spend much of his life asking "Who am I?" because it had been answered for him. He found in God not a love that recognized value, but instead a love that gave value. His value was a gift, and therefore, a given. God's answer, though often challenged, for him, was enough. After claiming that value for himself, he offered it to others.

The psychology of Jesus is based on value giving love that sees self and others as beloved. The challenge for us is to find that same sense of self-worth which enables us to live a full, Jesus-like life, and then share it with others as we search for ways to give value to others.

Reflection

Read the following. How do they relate to the passage and concepts above? Where do you see value recognizing and value giving love?

Romans 8: *For you did not receive a spirit of slavery to fall back into fear, but you have received a spirit of adoption. When we cry, "Abba! Father!"* [16] *it is that very Spirit bearing witness with our spirit that we are children of God,* [17] *and if children, then heirs, heirs of God and joint heirs with Christ.*

If Thou Must Love Me
by Elizabeth Barrett Browning
> *If thou must love me, let it be for naught*
> *Except for love's sake only. Do not say*
> *"I love her for her smile. . . her look. . . her way*
> *Of speaking gently.. .for a trick of thought*
> *That falls in well with mine, and certes brought*
> *A sense of pleasant ease on such a day"*
> *For these things in themselves, Belovéd, may*
> *Be changed, or change for thee, - and love, so wrought,*
> *May be unwrought so. Neither love me for*
> *Thine own dear pity's wiping my cheeks dry,*
> *A creature might forget to weep, who bore*
> *Thy comfort long, and lose thy love thereby!*
> *But love me for love's sake, that evermore*
> *Thou mayst love on, through love's eternity.*

Last Fragment
by Raymond Carver
> *And did you get what*
> *you wanted from this life, even so? I did.*
> *And what did you want?*
> *To call myself beloved, to feel myself beloved on the earth.*

Exercise

Who do you hold in highest regard? How do they shape your sense of self? What role does God play in your life?

What do you believe God believes about you?

If you are part of a church that baptizes babies, how significant for you is the declaration that you are a child of God before you are even aware of it? When you see a baptism, do you celebrate your own baptism affirming that you are beloved of God regardless of your attempts to prove it or earn it, regardless of what voices might tell you otherwise?

Read Raymond Carver's "Last Fragment" again.
> *And did you get what*
> *you wanted from this life, even so? I did.*
> *And what did you want?*
> *To call myself beloved, to feel myself beloved on the earth.*

When you get to the end of your life, will you be able to answer the questions in the same way as Carver? Why or why not?

List five times recently you have experienced being beloved. Who showed that love to you? Who defined you as loved?

Temptation of Christ
Vasily Surikov 1872

Overcome the devils
with a thing called love.
Bob Marley

Chapter Three: the devil

Primary Concept:
Before we can move forward into
a life of healthy relationships,
we must face challenges to our
sense of self-worth.

Voices. We encounter many in our lives. Some call us, "Beloved," while others question whether we have any value at all. Some build our sense of self-worth, while others challenge, question, or tear at it. At the onset of his ministry, Jesus encountered the voice of God at the Jordan River and then the voice of the devil in the desert. Whereas the voice of God affirmed Jesus' worth and value, the voice of the devil challenged and questioned it.

Countee Cullen wrote of one boy's encounter with a devilish voice in *Incident*.

Once riding in old Baltimore,
Heart-filled, head-filled with glee,
I saw a Baltimorean
Keep looking straight at me.

Now I was eight and very small,
And he was no whit bigger,
And so I smiled, but he poked out
His tongue, and called me, 'Nigger.'

I saw the whole of Baltimore
From May until December,
Of all the things that happened there
That's all that I remember.

Likely, the boy had voices in his life that had told him many times that he was loved, valuable, special, and important. Yet, in an instant, this voice of a stranger, this voice of someone the boy would never see again, shattered his sense of self-worth, stole his courage to reach out to others, and soured his experience of Baltimore. He heard one voice among many, yet one voice with great influence.

Read the following text. Imagine that you are Jesus. How does the voice of the devil sound? How is it like the voice the boy encountered in "Incident?" How does the voice call into question the 'beloved' label?

Text

Matthew 4: *Then Jesus was led up by the Spirit into the wilderness to be tempted by the devil. 2 He fasted forty days and forty nights, and afterwards he was famished. 3 The tempter came and said to him, "If you are the Son of God, command these stones to become loaves of bread." 4 But he answered, "It is written, 'One does not live by bread alone, but by every word that comes from the mouth of God.'"*

5 Then the devil took him to the holy city and placed him on the pinnacle of the temple, 6 saying to him, "If you are the Son of God, throw yourself down; for it is written,

'He will command his angels concerning you,'

and 'On their hands they will bear you up,

so that you will not dash your foot against a stone.'"

7 Jesus said to him, "Again it is written, 'Do not put the Lord your God to the test.'"

8 Again, the devil took him to a very high mountain and showed him all the kingdoms of the world and their splendor; 9 and he said to him, "All these I will give you, if you will fall down and worship me." 10 Jesus said to him, "Away with you, Satan! for it is written,

'Worship the Lord your God, and serve only him.'"

11 Then the devil left him, and suddenly angels came and waited on him.

Concept in the Text

Jesus did not wander into the desert; he was led, guided, directed by the Spirit for the specific purpose of meeting with the devil. Encountering the devil in the desert was part of Jesus' journey, part of the plan for him, part of his maturing into an adult. Before Jesus could go forward into his life, before he could live out a sense of purpose, before he could be useful to others, and before he could live productively in relationship, Jesus had to face this voice in the desert.

The voice challenged Jesus to prove his worth as a child of God, "*If you are* the Son of God," the devil urged, "*then* turn these stones to bread. Prove you are someone. Prove you are special by doing what no other can." Similarly, at the top of the temple, the devil said, "*If you are* the Son of God *then* throw yourself down in front of everyone, have angels catch you, and let everyone see how magnificent you are by doing something amazing." After Jesus successfully navigated the first two challenges, the devil encouraged Jesus to distance himself from the voice of God in the name of power. "All the kingdoms of the world I will give to you if you fall down and worship me. As once in power, you can help them, you can save them. After all, how can you help them if you are not in control?" Jesus again refused. After Jesus surpassed the challenges to prove, earn or justify the label of love he had received from God, confident, secure in a valued sense of self, he began his ministry.

Concept in Depth

In his observations about human development, Alfred Adler noted that life begins in a *minus situation*. As we move beyond infancy, we notice how small, dependent and incapable we are compared to our parents, older siblings, or others larger and more advanced than we are. Not long after we begin do we see that we are, in essence, born small in a land of giants. In response to this noted minus, we feel inferior. To be human is to experience this sense of deficiency in one form or another as Adler said, *To be human means to feel inferior.* For Adler, before we can successfully move into life goals and relationships, we must first come to terms with these feelings of inferiority.

Jesus' journey is our journey. Before we can successfully go forward into our lives, before we can live out a sense of purpose, before we can be useful to others, and before we can live productively in relationship, we must face a sense of minus, a sense of less than, a sense of inferiority. In Jesus' temptation in the desert, we see three symptoms of people who have gotten lost in their lack, lost in the dry land of deficit.

Symptom #1: If you feel inferior, you'll be tempted to prove your sense of self-worth by living a life of ease, free of all discomfort, pain, or suffering.

Fasting in the desert, Jesus was hungry. The devil then challenged Jesus to prove he was beloved of God by doing something miraculous and turning a stone to bread. Jesus was fasting in order to see deeper into himself, to learn more about who he was before going forward into his life. With fasting always comes discomfort. The discomfort is part of the lesson. The discomfort is the teacher. The devil encouraged Jesus to avoid the ache of fasting, "Don't be hungry. Get what you want right now! Turn the stone to bread and ease the pain. After all, if you are beloved of God, you shouldn't be struggling like this." For many of us, discomfort, pain, or suffering seem a threat to our self-worth. The belief is this, "If I am loved, I won't suffer. I won't experience pain. I won't experience any distress." Churches today often reinforce this belief saying, "If you believe, if you trust God and are faithful, God will *bless* you." Here, *bless* means give you a life free of discomfort or challenges.

Yet life is not that way. Life, by nature, is difficult. Consider this man who boarded a packed subway. The subway was so crowded that there was little room for him so he stood at the door looking out. The train started. He immediately regretted the spicy food he had for lunch as all the underground terrain sped by out the door in front of him. The blur, combined with the big burrito he had eaten earlier, made him nauseous and his head spin. When the train stopped and the doors opened, there was another crowd at the station. No one exited, and so no one could enter. While one crowd faced another, the nauseas passenger lost his lunch right there on another man standing at the platform. The two men stared at each other. Neither man moved. The door closed and the train pulled away. The man left on the platform was heard to say, "Why me?"

My response to the man, and to others when they ask, "Why me?" is this, "Why not you?" You are alive. Vomit happens. Vomit is not picky. Life includes throwing up and being thrown up on. People who ask, "Why me?" don't get it. Difficulty, pain, discomfort are not signs of unworthiness, devalue or lack of love. They are part of life. If Jesus had problems, why won't you? If Jesus was beloved and still struggled, why shouldn't you? Like with Jesus, it is not our pain that defines us but instead what we do with it. Scott Peck challenged us, like Jesus, to see discomfort as a gift. He said, *The truth is that our finest moments are most likely to occur when we are feeling deeply uncomfortable, unhappy, or unfulfilled. For it is only in such moments, propelled by our discomfort, that we are likely to step out of our ruts and start searching for different ways or truer answers.* Jesus' response to the devil was this, "It is written, 'One does not live by bread alone, but by every word that comes from the mouth of God.' " For Jesus, discomfort was not devalue, for Jesus discomfort was a doorway to something more. Jesus wanted something more and saw discomfort not as challenge to his self-worth but part of the common human experience.

Symptom #2: If you feel inferior, you'll be tempted to prove your sense of self-worth by being spectacular.

Alfred Adler said, *Behind everyone who behaves as if he were superior to others, we can suspect a feeling of inferiority which calls for very special efforts of concealment. It is as if a man feared that he was too small and walked on his toes to make himself seem taller.* For the second temptation in the gospel of Matthew, the devil took Jesus to the center of the capital city of Jerusalem, to the highest spot in the middle of town, to the top of the temple. What's significant about this high and central location is that, in contrast to the privacy of the desert, the devil urged Jesus to perform a public miracle for others to see.

When we don't have a strong sense of self, we will look to almost anyone to tell us we have value. The devil tempted Jesus here to see himself not through the eyes of God, but through the crowd. "Be impressive. Be amazing. Be spectacular. As soon as others see you up here, the crowd will gather and watch. When you jump off and angels save you, the crowd will know you are someone special." The devil seems to be a good observer of human nature knowing that when we feel inferior, we try and become spectacular so that others will tell us how amazing, how wonderful, how magnificent we are.

After worship at a church, a small boy stood behind the pulpit, pulled down the microphone, and shouted, "Look at me! Look at me!" One woman turned to another in her pew, "His father preaches that every Sunday."

"Look at me!" we shout. "See how special, spectacular, superior, I am." As Adler said, *Behind everyone who behaves as if he were superior to others, we can suspect a feeling of inferiority.*

Jesus' response to the devil was this, "Don't put the Lord your God to the test." In other words, "If God has called me beloved, who are you, or who am I, to question it?"

Symptom #3: If you feel inferior, you'll be tempted to prove your sense of self-worth by being in charge, in control, or dominating others.

Freud held that sex was the primary drive of human behavior. Alfred Adler disagreed. He saw in human behavior a search for power attributed to a sense of inferiority experienced in childhood. Adler observed there were two basic responses to the discovery of our inferiority, either we imitate our parents and assert our identity by trying to be in control and in charge, or we become more infantile in response to our sense of inferiority and try to use our extreme sense of need to get others to do for us what we want. He described how powerful the infantile approach can be by saying, *Tears and complaints—the means which I have called "water power"—can be an extremely useful weapon for disturbing cooperation and reducing others to a condition of slavery.* For Adler, acting like a dominating parent or imitating a helpless infant are both attempts at power and both unhealthy ways of dealing with our sense of inferiority.

In this third temptation of the devil, Jesus was urged to prove his self worth by parenting the world. "Deny the sense of self you received from God," the devil essentially tells Jesus, "bow to me, and I will give you power over the world – a world that terribly needs a Messiah, needs a Savior, needs you!" The desire to control others may deny others altogether or think only of others and ignore self. The desire to control the world may be cloaked in a worthy hope to save the world, the organization, the church, the family. Wanting to help others is a positive goal, however, when you believe that you are the only one who is capable of doing so, the only one that can save others, the origin is obviously from a weak sense of self trying to prove its value. Adler said, *One of the most interesting complexes is the redeemer complex. It characterizes people who conspicuously but unknowingly take the attitude that they must save or redeem someone. There are thousands of degrees and variations, but it is always clearly the attitude of a person who finds his superiority in solving the complications of others.*

Jesus' response to the devil was, "Worship the Lord your God, and serve only him." In other words, "If God has called me beloved; who would I be to bow to another?"

Application

Catholic priest and writer Henri Nouwen gave up his teaching position at Yale to serve handicapped adults at a residence facility in New England. Shortly before he was to lead a prayer service in one of the houses, Janet, a handicapped resident came to him and said, "Henri, can you give me a blessing?" Henri responded with a smile and traced the cross with his thumb on her forehead. She just stared back at him. "That didn't work," she said.

Henri looked at her for a moment, and then said, "How about I give you a real blessing when the whole group is together for the prayer service?" She smiled and nodded her head.

After the service with about thirty people sitting together in a circle, Henri said, "Janet has asked me to give her a special blessing. She feels that she could use one right now." Henri wasn't sure just what she needed or what he was going to do, but as soon as he said, "Janet has asked me to give her a special blessing," she stood up and walked to Henri. She wrapped her arms around him, put her head on his chest and gave him a big hug. Without thinking, Henri covered her with the long droopy sleeves of his minister's robe. Then Henri said, "Janet, I want you to know that you are God's beloved daughter. You are precious in God's eyes. Your beautiful smile, your kindness to the people in your house and all the good things you do show us what a beautiful human being you are. I know you feel a little low these days and that there is some sadness in your heart, but I want you to remember who you are: a very special person, deeply loved by God and all the people who are here with you."

As Henri finished these words, Janet raised her head and looked at him. Her broad smile was evidence that she had heard and received the blessing. When she sat back down, Jane, another resident, raised her hand and said, "I want a blessing, too." She stood up and, hugged Henri with her head against his chest. After he spoke blessings to her, many of the other residents wished to be blessed in the same way. Then one of the assistants, a twenty-four-year-old student, raised his hand and said, "What about me?"

"Sure," was Henri's reply. "Come." He came and Henri blessed him in the same way saying, "John, it is so good that you are here. You are God's beloved Son. Your presence is a joy for all of us. When things are hard and life is burdensome, always remember that you are loved with an everlasting love."

After Henri spoke, John looked at him with tears in his eyes and said, "Thank you, thank you very much."[vii]

Jesus overcame the challenge of inferiority, the devil voice's demand that he prove his worth. With nothing to attest, Jesus could bless others as he had been blessed, he could stand against all other voices and claim that no voice, devil or otherwise, could diminish what God has valued. No voice. Not even death.

I had just finished dinner one night when the phone rang. I was asked to go visit a couple in the hospital who didn't have a minister but would like to see one. They had been pregnant with their first child, 33 weeks along. She went to the doctor, and everything was fine. The next day things didn't feel right, she returned and to their horror, there was no heartbeat.

She was induced.

When I got there, they were still holding the body of their little girl. I introduced myself, and found out the name of the baby.

We talked for a little, but mostly we sat in quiet and looked at the body of their little girl.

The mother asked, "I don't suppose we could baptize her."

"Sure, we can," I replied.

I held the lifeless body in my arm and baptized her. I baptized her because I firmly trust the declaration of God. The baptism wasn't centered in a love that recognizes value, but a love that gives value. As I held the body in my arms, we prayed together entrusting the life of their daughter to God – that God would hold her – that God had already taken her in his arms and said, "My child."

I believe God's label is stronger than the label of her parents, stronger than the doctor who labeled her, "gone" or the coroner and the mortician who labeled her "dead". God's label was stronger than them all for God named her, "Mine.

My child. My beloved." I believe there is no naming stronger than God's naming. Not even death's. It is an act of faith. I cannot prove it. I can only trust. For me, in that trust is the freedom to move beyond "Who am I?" to let go of all diagnosing of what's wrong with me or what's wrong with you, to step away from whatever sense of inferiority I might have, to free myself from valuing myself or others in any way other than beloved.

Challenge for Us

The psychology of Jesus comes from a value giving love, a love that defines us and empowers us to see others as beloved.

When we try and live a life free from all difficulty, when we try and be spectacular so that others see us and tell us we are amazing, or when we try and control the world or save the world, we are living out of a devalued sense of self-worth trying to prove our value. Like Jesus, before we can go forward into our lives, we must address the devilish voice of inferiority that we find in our own personal dry lands, our own deserts. Jesus challenges us to see our self-value from a place of faith, a place of trust with no need to prove anything.

Once we have put the devilish voice of inferiority behind us, with a renewed sense of self-worth, we are freed from games to prove ourselves and empowered to live productive lives in healthy relationships.

Reflection

Real love is a permanently self-enlarging experience. – M. Scott Peck

Our dependency makes slaves out of us, especially if this dependency is a dependency of our self-esteem. If you need encouragement, praise, pats on the back from everybody, then you make everybody your judge. – Fritz Perls

The curious paradox is that when I accept myself just as I am, then I can change. – Carl Rogers

A thought transfixed me: for the first time in my life I saw the truth as it is set into song by so many poets, proclaimed as the final wisdom by so many thinkers. The truth— that love is the ultimate and the highest goal to which man can aspire. Then I grasped the meaning of the greatest secret that human poetry and human thought and belief have to impart: The salvation of man is through love and in love. – Viktor Frankl

Exercise

Think of the following challenges to your sense of self-worth. Can you think of a time when you tried to prove your value by:

- Avoiding pain?
- Being spectacular?
- Being in charge? the parent to the world? the savior?
- Denying your humanity? your mortality?

How would claiming your self-worth and the worth of others, as a gift from God empower you to go forward in your own life?

The Prodigal Son Driven Out
Bartolome Esteban Murillo 1660

As long as we continue to live as if we are what we do, what we have, and what other people think about us, we will remain filled with judgments, opinions, evaluations, and condemnations. We will remain addicted to putting people and things in their "right" place. -- Henri Nouwen

Chapter Four: Pharisees and the Scribes

Primary Concept:
*The psychology of Jesus focuses
more on location and movement
rather than identity and character.*

If you are familiar with the Bible, make a list of several people you remember from the gospels who encountered Jesus. Beside each name, write their locations if you can. Now put an asterisk by each location that gives significant information about the person.

Here is my list of people with tell-tale locations: Zacchaeus up a tree (Luke 19), the demoniac in the tombs (Mark 5), the lepers on the outside of town (Luke 17), the woman at the well in the middle of the day (John 4), Nicodemus who comes at night (John 3), Herod in Jerusalem (Matthew 2), Lazarus in his tomb (John 11), the disciples behind locked doors (John 20), Thomas away from the other disciples (John 20), and Peter and the other disciples returning to their boats (John 21). The list is not all-inclusive but enough to illustrate how the gospels use locations to tell us about people and how Jesus paid attention to location noting not only where people were but where they were relative to others. For example, it is not just that Zacchaeus is up a tree, but he is up a tree away from the crowd.

The next passage will be in three parts. In this first section, what is the tone the Pharisees use to speak of Jesus? Why do you think they don't speak to Jesus directly? What is their diagnosis of the people Jesus' dinner companions and of Jesus?

Text (Part One)

Luke 15: *Now all the tax collectors and sinners were coming near to listen to (Jesus). ² And the Pharisees and the scribes were grumbling and saying, "This fellow welcomes sinners and eats with them."*

Concept in the Text (Part One)

In this passage, the author contrasts Jesus and the Pharisees. The contrast is of thought and movement. The Pharisees think ill of the people with Jesus. The Pharisees diagnose them saying, "This fellow, (Jesus), welcomes *sinners* (people who were *trash* to use Freud's terms or *depraved* to use Calvin's) and eats with them." In the mind of the Pharisees and Scribes, to welcome a 'sinner,' as Jesus was doing, was to give them more respect than they deserved. To eat with them was to equate yourself with them – 'you are who you eat with.' Because Jesus welcomed 'sinners' (instead of condemning them) and ate with them (instead of separating himself from them) they pointed out that he must also be a sinner. The Pharisees, whose name means 'separate ones,' act true to form here as they separate from the others and from Jesus. They don't even speak *to* Jesus but *about* him, though they were probably loud enough for Jesus to hear.

Jesus does not argue with the Pharisees over their diagnoses of the character of those he is with or of him. Jesus does not speak about them as they spoke about him, but instead he speaks directly to them. Instead of condemning in tone and manner, Jesus is inviting. He moves toward them and offers, in three stories or parables, an alternative to their habit of diagnosing others. We'll look at the first two stories together.

Text (Part Two)

Luke 15: *3 So (Jesus) told them this parable: 4 "Which one of you, having a hundred sheep and losing one of them, does not leave the ninety-nine in the wilderness and go after the one that is lost until he finds it? 5 When he has found it, he lays it on his shoulders and rejoices. 6 And when he comes home, he calls together his friends and neighbors, saying to them, 'Rejoice with me, for I have found my sheep that was lost.' 7 Just so, I tell you, there will be more joy in heaven over one sinner who repents than over ninety-nine righteous persons who need no repentance.*

Or what woman having ten silver coins, if she loses one of them, does not light a lamp, sweep the house, and search carefully until she finds it? 9 When she has found it, she calls together her friends *and neighbors, saying, 'Rejoice with me, for I have found the coin that I had lost.' ¹⁰ Just so, I tell you, there is joy in the presence of the angels of God over one sinner who repents."*

Concept in the Text (Part Two)

In this first parable, Jesus doesn't diagnose or label the character of the sheep. He doesn't label the sheep as stupid, rebellious, or disobedient. He doesn't describe it as disruptive, wandering, or dull. There is nothing in the parable to distinguish the sheep from the other ninety-nine at all other than its location. To understand the sheep "Who is he?" doesn't give us any insight to the sheep's problem, but "Where is he?" clarifies much. The sheep is distant, separated, and lost. It should be with the rest of the sheep but instead it is out in the wilderness.

In the second parable, Jesus offers a similar illustration. The coin had no distinction from the other coins, no separating characteristic, no defect of note that caused or facilitated it being of less in value than the other coins. Like the sheep, it was separated and that was the issue.

Jesus offered these two parables and the next to discourage the diagnosing and labeling by the Pharisees (and by us) and to encourage them (and us) to pay attention to the location of the separated ones. For Jesus, the term 'sinner' is a diagnosis of distance rather than character. A 'sinner' is separated, not where he or she should be in relationship to God or others. Jesus reframes the term 'sinner' to be synonymous with 'lost,' a term of location not character.

Text (Part Three)

In the third parable, the younger son has been mislabeled and misdiagnosed more than anyone else in all of scripture. His label has barred us from understanding him (the way most labels bar us from understanding others). We call him "The Prodigal" (someone who is wasteful) because he squandered the family's money while his older brother stayed home and worked the farm (faithfully in our minds). We have judged the younger son 'bad' and the older 'good'. This labeling was never the intent of the parable, nor does it fit the psychology of Jesus. This is a story, as stated by the parable, of *a man who had two sons*. Both of the sons in the story, like the lost sheep and the lost coin, have distance issues. Read the following story. Note distances and movements.

Luke 15: *¹¹ Then Jesus said, "There was a man who had two sons. ¹² The younger of them said to his father, 'Father, give me the share of the property that will belong to me.' So he divided his property between them.*

¹³ A few days later the younger son gathered all he had and traveled to a distant country, and there he squandered his property in dissolute living. ¹⁴ When he had spent everything, a severe famine took place throughout that country, and he began to be in need. ¹⁵ So he went and hired himself out to one of the citizens of that country, who sent him to his fields to feed the pigs. ¹⁶ He would gladly have filled himself with the pods that the pigs were eating; and no one gave him anything. ¹⁷ But when he came to himself he said, 'How many of my father's hired hands have bread enough and to spare, but here I am dying of hunger! ¹⁸ I will get up and go to my father, and I will say to him, "Father, I have sinned against heaven and before you; ¹⁹ I am no longer worthy to be called your son; treat me like one of your hired hands." ' ²⁰ So he set off and went to his father.

But while he was still far off, his father saw him and was filled with compassion; he ran and put his arms around him and kissed him. ²¹ Then the son said to him, 'Father, I have sinned against heaven and before you; I am no longer worthy to be called your son.'

²² But the father said to his slaves, 'Quickly, bring out a robe—the best one—and put it on him; put a ring on his finger and sandals on his feet. ²³ And get the fatted calf and kill it, and let us eat and celebrate; ²⁴ for this son of mine was dead and is alive again; he was lost and is found!' And they began to celebrate.

"Now his elder son was in the field; and when he came and approached the house, he heard music and dancing. ²⁶ He called one of the slaves and asked what was going on.

²⁷ He replied, 'Your brother has come, and your father has killed the fatted calf, because he has got him back safe and sound.'

28 Then he became angry and refused to go in. His father came out and began to plead with him. 29 But he answered his father, 'Listen! For all these years I have been working like a slave for you, and I have never disobeyed your command; yet you have never given me even a young goat so that I might celebrate with my friends. 30 But when this son of yours came back, who has devoured your property with prostitutes, you killed the fatted calf for him!'

31 Then the father said to him, 'Son, you are always with me, and all that is mine is yours. 32 But we had to celebrate and rejoice, because this brother of yours was dead and has come to life; he was lost and has been found.'"

In the beginning of the story, the younger son moves away from the family. He shows his distance from his father by asking for his inheritance early. He says, in essence, "It would be better for me, father, if you were dead. But since you're not, can I have my inheritance now rather than waiting for you to die?" To our surprise, the father grants his request and the son moves away (though he was obviously already distant from father and family before he left home).

He spends the money, and once the wealth is gone, the younger brother repents (or turns back) toward home. "Who am I?" becomes focal for him, *I will get up and go to my father, and I will say to him, "Father, I have sinned against heaven and before you; 19 I am no longer worthy to be called your son; treat me like one of your hired hands."* Though primary for the son as he sees himself as *no longer worthy,* the father is no more concerned over his son's sense of self than the shepherd who lost his sheep or woman who lost her coin were in the identity of the sheep or the coin. Like them, the father is only glad upon the son's return. He had been watching for his son to come home. When he sees the boy, while the boy is still far off, the father moves toward him. In his movement, he lets everybody know that this boy is not disowned but is still his son, his beloved. The movement of the father communicates the identity for all to see. The son is, as he always was, valued and beloved.

Like his younger brother, the elder is also distant. He is also where he shouldn't be – away from the Father. Also like his younger brother, he doesn't consider himself worthy to be a son either. He says, *Listen! For all these years I have been working like a slave for you, and I have never disobeyed your command...* Command? You don't command sons, you command slaves. He sees himself as a less-than, a slave, rather than beloved son. His complaint, *yet you have never given me even a young goat so that I might celebrate with my friends* shows his distance. He doesn't want to celebrate with his father and the family, but his friends alone. How he labels his brother also shows distance, *30 But when this son of yours* (not 'my brother') *came back, who has devoured your property with prostitutes* (there is nothing in the story about prostitutes, he adds this in condemnation)*, you killed the fatted calf for him!'*

Jesus offers the older brother in this parable as an invitation to the Pharisees and the Sadducees. Like the elder brother, they are distant from the 'sinners' Jesus was eating with. We see ourselves in the elder brother, anytime we belittle others we do not reveal their character but our own distance from them, and anytime we belittle others, we show our own lack of a sense of value in ourselves as loved.

Both brothers were away from where they should be. Both brothers understood themselves as 'less than' terms, all the while the father in the story was showing that there is no question of identity – they are valued, loved, not less-than at all. Their problem was simple – distance.

Jesus ends the story with the older brother's location away from the party and his movement undecided. Jesus uses the parable to offer the 'separate ones' a chance to move toward others.

Application

Perhaps there is no better example of the deficiency of the "Who am I?" question than with wondering "Who is God?" People have debated for thousands of years with libraries full of volumes and churches full of creeds. However, those answers aren't near as helpful as asking "Where is God?" and "Where is God going?"

Belief in God or gods was not new for Israel at the composition of the Hebrew Scriptures (which Christians call the Old Testament). There were temples, there were altars, but gods were typically deities of location, confined to areas. The story of Abram tells of a God who moves. He travels with Abram and later with Israel. The profession of monotheists was that not only was there one God, but this God was not confined to space but moved. Images of God were shaped around how God moves. Consider the parables mentioned earlier. God is imaged as a shepherd, a woman, and a father. Movement tells us more about the images of God than just the image alone. God is like a shepherd, is not near as helpful as, God is like a shepherd who moves toward his lost sheep until he finds them and brings them back home. When we look at movement, not only do those three parables open up, but so does the whole Bible.

In the beginning, Genesis 1 the earth is full of water and chaos and the spirit of God moves over the water. Chapter two, God's children disobey and run away and hide. God moves toward them. They are thrown out of the garden. God moves with them. In Egypt, Israel is in slavery. God moves toward them and delivers them. Throughout their history, they run away from God, God moves toward them. At Christmas, God moves toward us in Jesus. We kill him. He's dead. God moves toward us still. God doesn't just move – God moves toward us, and there is nothing that can get in God's way!

At Easter, the disciples, behind locked doors, Mary, blinded by her grief, God in Christ moves toward them all. He moves boulders, through walls, into graves. God moves. Regardless of where we are or what walls we build, no matter whether we hide ourselves or others bury us – God moves toward us. As Paul wrote in Romans 8, my paraphrase in parenthesis, *If God (moves toward us), who (can move) against us? (Who can stand in God's way?)... I am convinced that neither death, nor life, nor angels, nor rulers, nor things present, nor things to come, nor powers, 39 nor height, nor depth, nor anything else in all creation, will be able to separate us from the love of God in Christ Jesus our Lord.*

Not only does the Bible present the story of a God who moves, but also a God who sends. In the early stories of the Bible, God calls Abram to go from his home and head to a land of promise. His grandson, Jacob, separates from his bother Essau, but God keeps sending him back home. Joseph's brothers separate themselves from him by selling him into slavery in Egypt. Through the use of a famine, God sends these brothers who would be separate toward Joseph in Egypt. Moses leaves Egypt in fear for his life after killing an Egyptian. He finds safety tending another man's flocks. God sends him back to Egypt. Example upon example exists throughout scripture of us separating and God sending, we divide,

God unites.

God moves. God sends.

Challenge for Us

Jesus attends to movement. He likens himself to a shepherd who moves freely to try and bring the distant back home. The challenge for us is to stop diagnosing others as sinners, as defective, and recognize distance. The challenge for us is to bridge the distances that divide us (like the shepherd of the parable) and to always offer hospitality, a welcoming home (like the father of the parable for both his children).

Reflection

The question is not "How am I to find God?" but "How am I to let myself be found by him?" The question is not "How am I to know God?" but "How am I to let myself be known by God?" And, finally, the question is not "How am I to love God?" but "How am I to let myself be loved by God?" God is looking into the distance for me, trying to find me, and longing to bring me home. -Henri Nouwen

Never cease loving a person, and never give up hope for him, for even the prodigal son who had fallen most low, could still be saved; the bitterest enemy and also he who was your friend could again be your friend; love that has grown cold can kindle.
—Soren Kierkegaard

Grace is the celebration of life, relentlessly hounding all the non-celebrants in the world. It is a floating, cosmic bash shouting its way through the streets of the universe, flinging the sweetness of its cassations to every window, pounding at every door in a hilarity beyond all liking and happening, until the prodigals come out at last and dance, and the elder brothers finally take their fingers out of their ears. —Robert Farrar Capon

Exercise

Make a list of people you have labeled negatively. Are you distant from them? In what ways?

How have you given them a label other than loved? How does the label show the distance?

What would happen if you moved toward them? Has God been sending you toward them? Has God given you the opportunity to make contact you haven't taken? What would happen if you tried to make contact? What frightens you? What gives you hope?

Think back over your own history, were there times in your life you felt close to God? distant? Where are you now? Is God pursuing you now? Are you pursuing God?

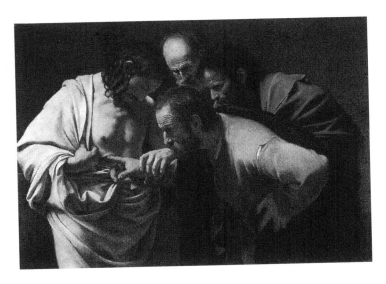

The Incredulity of Saint Thomas
Amerighi da Caravaggio 1601

When I get honest, I admit I am a bundle of paradoxes. I believe and I doubt, I hope and get discouraged, I love and I hate, I feel bad about feeling good, I feel guilty about not feeling guilty. I am trusting and suspicious. I am honest and I still play games. Aristotle said I am a rational animal; I say I am an angel with an incredible capacity for beer. Brennan Manning

Chapter Five: Thomas

Primary Concept:
Better than "Who am I?" and
"What's wrong with me?"
are the questions,
"Where am I?" and
"Where am I going?"

In Austria in 1902, a group of men, mostly doctors and all Jewish, began meeting every Wednesday in an apartment in Vienna. They called themselves the *Wednesday Society* and were led by Sigmund Freud. Later, they changed the name to *The Vienna Psychoanalytical Society* and elected Alfred Adler as president. In 1911, a group split off when Adler chose a different approach to psychology than Freud. [viii] Whereas Freud looked closely at a patient's past, Adler examined the person's present. Whereas Freud explored a patient's subconscious drives, Adler looked at a person's conscious choices. And, most importantly, whereas Freud concentrated on a patient's desires, Adler examined a person's movement. *Trust only movement,* Adler said. *Life happens at the level of events, not of words. Trust movement.* Adler wrote that movement makes us alive, and social movement makes us human. According to Adler, *We attribute a soul only to moving, living organisms. The soul stands in innate relationship to free motion. Those organisms which are strongly rooted have no necessity for a soul. How supernatural it would be to attribute emotions and thoughts to a deeply rooted plant!*

Though Freud's approach is more widely known, Adler's method gives us more insight into how Jesus treated people, especially those with problems. Consistently, Jesus did not diagnose others, but instead examined location, distance and movement. He cared less about what and how a person thought, and more about how he or she related to others. There is perhaps no character better to illustrate Jesus' approach than how he related to Thomas, the disciple. We, through the centuries, have diagnosed Thomas giving him the label, "Doubting Thomas." We have held Thomas up as an example not to follow, "Don't be a Doubting Thomas."

Unfortunately, in our diagnosis, we have closed our eyes to the person. However, by avoiding the traditional diagnostic approach to Thomas and instead choosing location-centered examination, by asking not "Who is he?" or "What's wrong with him?" and instead asking "Where is he?" and "Where is he going (or moving)?" we can learn a lot about Thomas and ourselves that we have missed for centuries.

Read through this second part of the Easter story. Look not for fault in Thomas, defect in his character or nature, but instead look at his location, his distance, and his movement.

Text

John 20: *19 When it was evening on that day, the first day of the week, and the doors of the house where the disciples had met were locked for fear of the Jews, Jesus came and stood among them and said, "Peace be with you." 20 After he said this, he showed them his hands and his side. Then the disciples rejoiced when they saw the Lord. 21 Jesus said to them again, "Peace be with you. As the Father has sent me, so I send you."*

22 When he had said this, he breathed on them and said to them, "Receive the Holy Spirit. 23 If you forgive the sins of any, they are forgiven them; if you retain the sins of any, they are retained."

24 But Thomas (who was called the Twin), one of the twelve, was not with them when Jesus came. 25 So the other disciples told him, "We have seen the Lord."

But he said to them, "Unless I see the mark of the nails in his hands, and put my finger in the mark of the nails and my hand in his side, I will not believe."

26 A week later his disciples were again in the house, and Thomas was with them. Although the doors were shut, Jesus came and stood among them and said, "Peace be with you."

27 Then he said to Thomas, "Put your finger here and see my hands. Reach out your hand and put it in my side. Do not doubt but believe."

28 Thomas answered him, "My Lord and my God!"

Concept in the Text

One of the first things we learn about Thomas in this passage is that he was not an only child. He had at least one sibling for he was a twin (v.24).

Twins, more so than the rest of us, are very sensitive to distance and movement. I talked to a pastor friend, Paul Burns, who is twin. Here is how he described being a twin. He said, "When I was an infant, barely able to crawl, I would always look for my brother. If I was playing, and suddenly realized my brother wasn't in the room, I would become anxious. I would say, 'Where David?' My brother would do the same thing. 'Where Paul? Where Paul?' Our childhood was like that. We were always together. As a child, I didn't like the separation. When we were apart, I would miss him. I would feel like part of me was missing."

A parent at my church told me about his daughters. In preschool, when they were learning the alphabet, his twins would divide the letters. Nina would say to Madison as they looked at the alphabet letters trying to recall the letters, "That's the one you know."

I asked a twin in my church, Maggie, to tell me what the experience of having an identical sister has been like for her. She said, "For me being a twin means I'm seldom alone. It's always been that way, ever since I was born. Genna's my twin and she's always been there. We like a lot of the same things, so we tend to do the same things. It's like, I would do something that I like and Genna would like it too. So we just do things together and it makes it fun. As a twin, shopping is great; I try on one outfit, she the other and I know how I'll look. Genna is not just my twin. She's my best friend; someone who laughs at my jokes, makes me laugh, says the right things right and is always there."

Twins aren't used to being alone. All children experience separation anxiety. The fear of being disconnected from a parent is normal. In a healthy relationship, parents go away. The child experiences the distance from the parent. The parent returns. Twins don't experience the concern over separation in the same way. They are usually left with the other. Whereas an oldest or only child would be left with another adult, the twin would be left with another adult and their twin. They don't experience the same separation feeling as other children. As a result, twins have a different sensitivity to separation. Paul Burns (the twin) pointed out to me how this helps us understand Thomas' behavior earlier in the Gospel of John. In John 11, Jesus told the disciples that he was going to Bethany where Lazarus lived. The disciples told Jesus that if he went near Jerusalem, where Bethany was, the leaders there would probably kill him. The disciples didn't want to go, but Thomas said, "If he's going there to die, let's go with him." Thomas couldn't stand the idea of being separated. He didn't want to be without Jesus even if it meant putting his own life in danger. So, wherever Jesus went, Thomas would go.

In John 14, Jesus told the disciples "I am going to prepare a place for you," talking about heaven, and very mysteriously, Jesus says, "You know where I am going." Thomas, very disturbed at this idea of separation from Jesus, spoke up, "We don't know where you're going! How can we? Tell us, we will go with you." To avoid separation, Thomas would follow Jesus anywhere.

Thomas' pain in the passage is distance felt. Jesus had gone somewhere Thomas couldn't follow. Grief, for Thomas and for us, after the death of someone we love, is pain caused by separation. We actually feel the distance. Thomas, as a twin, was likely more sensitive to the pain of the distance from Jesus after his death than the other disciples. As a result, Thomas, in his grief, didn't want to hurt any more. Protecting himself, he distanced himself from others. To be with the group only reminded him of his pain. When he returned to the group, even though his friends told him Jesus was alive, Thomas couldn't imagine it. Their word alone wasn't enough to cross the distance or ease his grief. "Unless I see the mark of the nails in his hands, and put my finger in the mark of the nails and my hand in his side, I will not believe." Unless Jesus was near enough for him to touch, he wouldn't believe. For Thomas, doubt wasn't a character problem, it was a distance problem. Understand the distance, understand the pain. Understand the pain, understand the behavior.

Concept in Depth

When we focus too much energy, as have the fields of theology and psychology, on the questions of "Who am I?" and "What's wrong with me?" then we easily label someone like Thomas as less than, as deficient, as wrong. Again, that's an unhelpful orientation. A better, healthier orientation is to examine not his character but his location and his movement. As Adler said, *Life happens at the level of events, not of words. Trust movement.*

To begin thinking of others in Jesus' way examining location and distance is not difficult. Our minds already think in these terms as evidenced by the metaphors we use when talking about relationships:

Location metaphors:
> *I have a special place in my heart for you.*
> *She is my closest friend.*
> *He's out of touch.*
> *She's out of reach.*
> *He needs room to grow.*
> *She's an outsider.*
> *Politically, you are on the far right.*
> *You're definitely to the left of me.*
> *You're outside the lines.*
> *You're on the edge of trouble.*

Movement metaphors:
> *We are going in circles.*
> *We are growing distant.*
> *You drive me crazy.*
> *You move too fast.*
> *You've slowed down a lot.*
> *He's on the journey toward becoming a man.*
> *She's climbing the ladder to success.*
> *He's following in his father's footsteps.*
> *She caught him.*
> *He did an about face, a U-turn.*
> *That was a step in the right direction.*
> *They are now on the road to a happy place.*

These and other metaphors show that we think and speak of ourselves, other people, and our relationships in terms of location, distance and movement. A lot of helpful work is being done in psychology in these areas looking at what is between us rather than what is within us when we are facing a problem. For example, William Glasser began Reality Therapy with this perception: most human pain results from loneliness. For Glasser, like Adler, when you are hurting, don't look at what's wrong with who you are but what's wrong with where you are. Don't look at your history, look at your present movement and ask, "Are you moving closer to others or away?"

With Thomas the disciple, two thousand years of asking "What was wrong with him?" and answering "Doubt" has not been helpful for us in learning about Thomas or ourselves. But when we examine his movement and understand that it was motivated out of pain, we gain a greater understanding of Thomas and human grief, including our own grief. Simply looking at location, distance and movement helps us understand a lot about Thomas, and it helps us understand a lot about ourselves and others.

When someone comes to see me as their pastor, bringing some personal pain seeking help, I listen for distance in their relationships. I listen for distance in one of these four areas: family, friends, work relationships, or God. Usually, when someone is feeling emotional pain, there is a distance problem in one or more of those four areas of relationships.

By listening for distance, I have had some positive results. One family I worked with in Georgia had a recurring medical issue with their son. About three months earlier, he had been injured in a football game. He took a hard blow to his mid section. A couple of days after the game, he seemed fine. A week later he had a relapse. He wouldn't eat. He continually complained of stomach pain. He lost weight. They took him to several doctors, ran scan after scan, but they couldn't find a source for his stomach problems. They were scheduled to see a specialist several hours away at a medical university when I went to see them. The mother, Sharon, and son, Darryl, were having some difficulty in their relationship and had invited me over to talk about it. I sat in the kitchen with both of them. I was surprised to see how much weight Darryl had lost and how much smaller he looked.

The older brother, Rick, was away for his freshman year in college. The father, Richard, was away on work. His former company had downsized his position a year earlier. Unable to find comparable work locally, he took a job in New York. He had been working there for six months coming home every other weekend.

I asked Sharon about Richard's job, when he was last home, and how the elder son, Rick, was doing in college. Then I asked Sharon and Darryl how they were doing living together with the older brother at school and father in New York.

"I'm so frustrated with Darryl," Sharon told me. Darryl said nothing. "In what way?" I asked.

"I just don't feel respected or appreciated," she said.

"Can you give me an example?" I asked.

"He comes home from school every day, goes straight to his room. I can't get him to talk to me. I've been taking care of the house, the dogs, and doing errands for the family all day. When evening comes, I want some company. I'm tired of being alone. I want someone to talk to. I want someone to listen about my day and talk to me, but when I ask him how his day was all he can say is, 'Fine' then he's off to his room leaving me alone. I need more than just 'fine.' I want some attention."

I said nothing. Darryl spoke up. "I don't want to tell her about my day. I've had a rough day at school. When I come home, I need a little peace and quiet before I can deal with family."

We sat quietly for a moment. Both of them looked at me, "So," I summed up, "Sharon, you want Darryl to tell you about his day, and Darryl, you want your mom to give you some space when you go home."

"Yes," they said in unison.

I waited. Then I asked. "How long has Richard been working in New York?" "Six months," she said.

"You miss him?" I asked.

"Yes," she said puzzled.

"I can hear it," I said. "When Richard was working in town, what was your end of the day routine?"

"Well," she said, "when he didn't have a meeting, he'd come home around six, and we'd each have a glass of wine and talk while I finished making dinner."

"Hmm," I said. "You miss that time. Since Richard isn't here to talk to you in the evening, you'd like for Darryl to give you some attention?"

"Yes," she said.

"The language you used about your problem communicating together is nothing unusual. It's just usually language a wife uses about her husband, or a husband about his wife, depending on who works away from the home. 'He doesn't talk to me when he gets home' isn't usually used from a mother about her son in the same way. With Richard gone, are you looking to Darryl to fill a little bit of his role?"

"I guess so," she said. "I just miss having Richard around, especially in the evening, and so I've been trying to get Darryl to talk to me."

"Then call dad," Darryl added.

"You haven't offered him the nightly glass of wine, yet, have you?" I asked. "Do you think it would help?" she laughed.

Darryl didn't think it was funny. I went over some ways they could talk to each other and relate to each other that would feel more like mother and son than husband and wife. I was at their house about an hour.

A couple of weeks later, I followed up and asked about Darryl's trip to the specialist. Sharon told me that Darryl had stopped complaining about his stomach, started eating, and was looking healthy again. They canceled the visit. Darryl had signed up for basketball.

Though a lot of youth are injured in sports, in this instance, the symptoms Darryl faced were not a result of physical injury, but his symptoms served a purpose in his relationship with his mother. Though Darryl's physical ailment was the focal point of the family's anxiety, he was only, what family systems therapists refer to as the role of the identified patient. The real problem was in an imbalance in their relationship which showed up in the son's mysterious physical symptoms. With dad away, mom had moved closer toward her son as companion. The shift in their relationship, and in his role, made the son uncomfortable. He did not want to fill out his father's absent role. When he first had his injury, his mother treated him less like a spouse and more like a son, as she took care of her child, not expecting him to fill his father's shoes. His injury restored their relationship to its former place. When he started to recover, the mother/son relationships started disappearing, so he relapsed to restore the balance he was used to. For Darryl, no doubt the pain and discomfort he felt were real, but as the doctors' tests showed, the problem's origin wasn't physical. The symptom served a purpose. It kept their relationship in check. In this case, as in many others, diagnosing the mother's problem or the son's symptom wouldn't help, examining their locations and movements did.

Challenge for Us

Our two thousand year old judgment of Thomas as a doubter shows us our tendency to diagnose others. The psychology of Jesus encourages more compassion. Instead of diagnosing character flaws, Jesus examines separation, distances, and movements toward and away from others.

The challenge for us from the psychology of Jesus is to follow his approach looking at distances trusting that more healing comes from movement than judgment.

Reflection

Read the following quotes. How do they relate to the passage and concepts above?

Love is reverence; it keeps its distance even as it draws near; it does not seek to absorb the other in the self or want to be absorbed by it. – Richard Niebuhr

Immature love says: 'I love you because I need you.' Mature love says 'I need you because I love you.' – Erich Fromm

Communication leads to community, that is, to understanding, intimacy and mutual valuing. – Rollo May

Exercise

List the significant relationships in your life. Define them in terms of closeness and distance. Is there pain or joy in those relationships relative to the proximity or distance you feel in the relationship? What movement do you see? Where do you see potential for movement?

How do you feel about moving toward someone you are currently distant from? Hopeful? Encouraged? Afraid? Angry?

Good Samaritan
Vincent Van Gogh

Life happens at the level of events, not of words.
Trust movement.
– Alfred Adler

Chapter Six: Zacchaeus

Primary Concept:
*We make choices based on our goals.
To understand our own behavior and the behaviors of
others, we must understand the underlying goals behind
our choices and actions.*

In second grade, I liked a girl named Tammy. One of the things I liked about Tammy was that she constantly told me who I was. If I was struggling with the "Who am I?" question, Tammy was more than happy to answer it for me. For example, Tammy and I had a disagreement over how to spell 'phone.' "You're crazy!" I told her. "There is no way that phone begins with a 'p'." We took our debate to the teacher, who, as the ultimate authority on all things phonetic, set me straight. "You're a terribly bad speller," she told me when we returned to our table. "Who am I?" The message was clear from Tammy, "I am a bad speller. That's who I am." We got back our math tests. She got a 75, and I got 100. "You are a math brain," she said. "Who am I?" "I am a math brain. That's who I am."

Tammy taught me that my identity came from my successes and my failures, my abilities and my deficiencies. She taught me that I am what I do. I didn't misspell 'phone,' I am a bad speller. I didn't make an 'A' on my math test, I am a math brain. This lesson was reinforced at home. If I didn't clean up my room, I was messy. If I didn't do my homework but watched TV, I was lazy. If I argued with my sister, I was mean.

The lessons continued into adulthood. Smoke and I am a smoker. Overdraw my checking account and I am irresponsible. Drink too much once and I am al,so irresponsible. Drink too much on several occasions and I am a drunk. Sleep with somebody because I feel lonely, and I am a slut. A very simple psychology: *actions = identity*, do good and you are a good person, do bad and you are a bad person.

This is the psychology the crowd has in the following scripture passage. Read the text. Imagine you are in the crowd. How do you judge Zacchaeus based on his actions? Read the text again and imagine you are Jesus. How do you see Zacchaeus differently than the crowd?

Text

Luke 19: *(Jesus) entered Jericho and was passing through it. ² A man was there named Zacchaeus; he was a chief tax collector and was rich. ³ He was trying to see who Jesus was, but on account of the crowd he could not, because he was short in stature. ⁴ So he ran ahead and climbed a sycamore tree to see him, because (Jesus) was going to pass that way.*

⁵ When Jesus came to the place, he looked up and said to him, "Zacchaeus, hurry and come down; for I must stay at your house today." ⁶ So he hurried down and was happy to welcome him.

⁷ All who saw it began to grumble and said, "He has gone to be the guest of one who is a sinner."

⁸ Zacchaeus stood there and said to the Lord, "Look, half of my possessions, Lord, I will give to the poor; and if I have defrauded anyone of anything, I will pay back four times as much."

⁹ Then Jesus said to him, "Today salvation has come to this house, because he too is a son of Abraham. ¹⁰ For the Son of Man came to seek out and to save the lost."

Concept in the Text

Zacchaeus' community diagnosed him through the eyes of an *actions = identity* psychology. The assumption is clear in the viewpoint: good people do good things, bad people do bad things, do good things and you are a good person, do bad things and you are a bad person. For the crowd, Zacchaeus did bad things because he was a bad person. Zacchaeus collected taxes for the Romans, he was a traitor. He took more than required, so he was a cheat. He worked with Gentiles instead of keeping the race pure, so he was unclean. He was, all in all, through the culminations of his actions, a sinner. They judged Jesus through the same lens, because Jesus ate with sinners, he was a sinner. You are what you do.

Jesus did not share their psychology. Jesus did not equate others with their actions. Jesus (on another occasion) said, "Judge not lest ye be judged." Why? Because he knew the game. As soon as you try and define who somebody is because of their actions, somebody is going to start doing the same to you.

Jesus looked at location, separation, and movement. Jesus saw Zacchaeus for where he was, up a tree, and how he got there. He didn't diagnose his character but his location.

Concept in Depth

Freud and Adler disagreed on the root source of human behavior. Freud believed that people were driven by conflicting internal processes, two drives (sex and aggression) which could seldom be satisfied, and divided personalities (id, ego, and superego) which were constantly at odds. Adler took a different approach which is illustrated in the following riddles.

Why did the banana go to the doctor?
Because he was not peeling well.

Why did the cookie go to the doctor?
Because he was feeling crummy.

Why did the boy tiptoe toward the medicine cabinet?
Because he didn't want to wake the sleeping pills.

Why didn't the lady run from the lion?
Because people told her it was a man eating lion.

Why was 6 afraid of 7?
Because 7 8 (ate) 9.

What do all these riddles have in common? Each presents a puzzling behavior: bananas and cookies going to the doctor, a boy tiptoes in the bathroom, a lady who doesn't run from a lion, and one number afraid of another, and then each riddle explains the behavior by revealing the motivation. *Why didn't the lady run from the lion? She didn't run because she thought the lion only ate men since it was a man eating lion.* Her assumption doesn't have to be correct to illuminate the behavior.

These riddles give a puzzling behavior and explain it. The best example is the oldest known riddle, *Why did the chicken cross the road? To get to the other side.* In the riddle, understand the goal, understand the mysterious actions. For human behavior, once we understand a person's goal, we understand the puzzle of a person's behavior.

Whereas Freud believed behavior was pushed by drives, Adler believed behavior was pulled by goals. Adler said it this way, *When we know the goal of a person, we know approximately what will follow.* Adler believed, *Each of us values only that which is appropriate to his goal. A real understanding of the behavior of any human being is impossible without a clear comprehension of the secret goal which he is pursuing; nor can we evaluate every aspect of his behavior until we know that his whole activity has been influenced by his goal.*

Why did Zacchaeus climb the tree? *He climbed up in the sycamore tree, for the Lord he wanted to see...* The children's song is clear; he climbed the tree because he wanted to see Jesus. If we didn't understand that Jesus was in town, if we didn't know that there was a crowd which blocked Zacchaeus's view of Jesus, we might question the behavior, "Why is that grown man climbing a tree?" But because we understand his goal, we understand his behavior.

Looking a little deeper, why was Zacchaeus a tax collector? We can't say for sure, but we can apply the same principal. We can assume that like climbing the tree, Zacchaeus had a motivation for being a tax collector which made sense to him. There must have been some benefits obvious to Zacchaeus about being a tax collector which made the choice attractive. Perhaps he thought collecting taxes for Rome would give him power, authority, wealth, or connections, no one knows for sure. For whatever reason, within the goals Zacchaeus set for himself, being a tax collector made sense to him at some point in his life.

The text tells us that to some extent, Zacchaeus had been successful as a tax collector. "...he was a chief tax collector and was rich." Yet, Zacchaeus wasn't satisfied. He wanted something more. Becoming a tax collector hadn't given him what he wanted. Zacchaeus had a faulty stategy. Zacchaeus probably would have agreed with Stephen Covey when he said, *It is incredibly easy to get caught up in an activity trap, in the busy-ness of life, to work harder and harder at climbing the ladder of success only to discover it's leaning against the wrong wall. It is possible to be busy — very busy — without being very effective.*

Looking for something more, he wanted to see Jesus. He needed to keep a safe distance between himself and the crowd, and between himself and Jesus, so he climbed a tree.

The crowd paid no attention to Zacchaeus' motivation. They only judged his character. To them, he did bad things because he was bad. Bad actions come from bad people.

Jesus doesn't judge Zacchaeus's character, he discerns his actions. I imagine the encounter went something like this:

Jesus, walking down the street, through the crowd, looks up and sees Zacchaeus in the tree. "Zacchaeus, what are you doing up in that tree?"

Zacchaeus is startled by three things. Jesus sees him. Jesus knows his name, and Jesus speaks his name as if he were a friend he hadn't seen in a while. "Zacchaeus, what are you doing up in that tree?" Jesus asks again.

"I wanted to see you, but I couldn't for the crowd. I climbed the tree so that I could see you."

"And...?" Jesus asks.

"And...?" Zacchaeus responds.

"Why else did you climb the tree?" Jesus pushes.

"I climbed the tree," Zacchaeus adds, "so that others wouldn't see me. I wanted to be away from the people."

"So that others wouldn't see you?" Jesus questions. He looks around the crowd. Those that weren't looking at him were looking at Zacchaeus. "How's that working for you?"

"Not very well," he admits.

"Well," Jesus says, "you wanted to see me, come down. I am going to come to your house." Zacchaeus' heart races. 'He spoke my name! He's coming to my house!'

At his home, the two men sit together with others gathering around. The crowd from the street has gathered within and outside Zacchaeus' home. Jesus says to Zacchaeus, "You chose to be a tax collector. Tell me about that choice. What were you looking for? Why did that make sense to you at the time?"

"I thought it would give me status. Make me a powerful person in the community. Get me respect from others."

Outside the crowd grumbles, "Why is Jesus eating at the home of a sinner?" Zacchaeus thinks of his life over the past few years.

Jesus asks, "So, how's that working for you?"

"Not very well," Zacchaeus admits.

Then Zacchaeus offers, "Look, half of my possessions, Lord, I will give to the poor; and if I have defrauded anyone of anything, I will pay back four times as much."

Jesus then points to Zacchaeus and speaks to the crowd, "Today salvation has come to this house, because he too is a son of Abraham... My primary purpose is to seek out and to save those who are lost."

Salvation came to Zacchaeus' house. Zacchaeus was saved, but saved from what?

The answer, I think, is in Zacchaeus' action. He responds to this salvation by becoming responsible. He says, "Look, half of my possessions, Lord, I will give to the poor; and if I have defrauded anyone of anything, I will pay back four times as much." Given Jesus' response and the stance of the text, I think we can assume that this is no idle promise. This is a sign of transformation. So, what is different? What is Zacchaeus delivered from?

In a word, shame. There was no sign of Zacchaeus taking responsibility for his actions before meeting Jesus. The reason is easy to understand. Before his encounter with Jesus, he lived under the oppression of an *actions=identity* psychology. With that mindset, shame dominates. The strength of shame comes from the combination of shame and guilt. In an *actions =identity* psychology, if you do bad then you are bad. Under the oppression of this mindset, few are able to absorb the shameful implication of mistakes, misgivings, errors, or flaws. The pain is so great. *Action=identity* psychology is rooted in a value recognizing love. The chief symptoms are: shame and guilt are identical; responsibility is painful; and any sign of weakness, flaw or error shows a defective, deficient, depraved soul. "He is a sinner," the crowd judged.

Jesus showed him a value giving love. This love frames Jesus' encounter with Zacchaeus. Jesus knows his name when they meet. He speaks it in love. He affirms him by eating at his home (to eat at someone's home is a sign of equality, if Jesus is God's beloved then he only eats with God's beloved). The encounter then ends with

Jesus calling Zacchaeus a "son of Abraham" (which means part of the community, child of God's calling, or child of God).

Jesus looks at Zacchaeus through the eyes of value giving love. Jesus saves him from the mind set of guilt (I did badly) and shame (I am bad) being the same. He saves him from his shame and liberates him to a new world of value giving love. Secure in his value, he is liberated and can then be responsible for his actions shame free. Zacchaeus finds a new world of possibility. Now able to own that his former strategy wasn't effective, he can look for another. While shame bound him to his past, Jesus interaction frees him to live in the present. He cannot change his yesterday, his previous choices and actions, but he can amend them in the present.

Application

Freed from shame and his past, Zacchaeus was enabled by Jesus to evaluate his choices by their effectiveness. Whether he was 'good' or 'bad', 'holy' or a 'sinner' became muted because at the center of his understanding of self, he saw himself as valuable, as loved. Though he had been called many names in the community, Jesus called him by his name. Though many voices rejected him, Jesus' voice claimed him and confirmed for him that he is a son of Abraham, or translated, child of God.

Choices and behavior are better understood from the perspective of goals and strategies. Like the riddles, understand the motivation, understand the behavior. As Adler said, *When we know the goal of a person, we know approximately what will follow.* Adler took this search for goals into some unexpected areas of human. Here are three places where understanding goals as motivators gives us insight to our behaviors and the behaviors of others in an evaluative but non judging approach.

Memories: Freud believed the answers to a patient's problems often resided in their past. For Freud, to understand the person, you must understand their formative past. For Adler, it wasn't the past which was as significant as what the person chose to remember from his or her history. Adler said, *Every memory, however trivial they may consider it, is important because by definition it represents to* *them something memorable, and it is memorable because of its bearing on life as they picture it. It says to them 'This is what you must expect', or 'This is what you must avoid,' or even 'Such is life!' Again we must stress that the experience itself is not as important as the fact that this particular experience persists in memory and is used to crystallize the meaning ascribed to life. Every memory is a chosen reminder.*

Adlerian counselors will often ask, "What is your first memory?" What they mean is, "Of all the experiences you had, what have you chosen to remember?" Those choices reveal often hidden goals and hidden worldviews.

One example Adler offers is a person who cited this as her first memory, "The coffee pot fell off the table and scalded me." Because she chose this as her first memory, Adler suggested that her world view would be that the world is a dangerous place and she is helpless in it. He also expected that she would frequently criticize others for not taking adequate care of her.

In churches, I ask leaders, "What's your first memory of being in a church?" Following Adler's lead, believing that we choose our first memories for a reason, I ask the leaders, "Why is that memory important to you?" "What do you see in that memory that a church should or shouldn't be?" "What do you want to create (or not create) at this church that you value from your first memory?" The discussions are often quite lengthy and full of insight.

Dreams: Whereas Freud and many others examined dreams for mystical allusions, Adler was much more practical. Adler looked away from universal symbols or connections and instead looked at the results of the dreams. Adler examined the emotions the dream aroused and the behaviors the emotions seemed to encourage. For Adler, in the dream, it is the emotions that matter. That is why, according to Adler, long after the dream images are gone, the emotions remain. You may awake from a dream in which you remember nothing except the emotion, but the emotion is usually ample for motivation.

For example, if you are facing a difficult decision and are unsure of what to do, if you go to bed and dream of flying, you likely awaken with a feeling that you can do something that didn't seem possible.

Your dream will give you encouragement (which you are seeking) to go forward unafraid. However, if facing that decision, you dream of flying then falling, your dream will give you discouragement (which you were looking for) to avoid the decision.

Adler shows how a dream may serve a specific behavior of a much broader goal. He gives the example of a man whose goal is to get money without working for it. He wants to buy a lottery ticket. He knows that others buy lottery tickets or gamble in other forms and fail. That night he dreams many people are jumping over a ditch. They all fail the jump and fall into the ditch. The man leaps it with ease. What do you think he did the next morning?

Love at "First Sight:" Though I haven't found this in Adler, it is a reasonable application. In each of us, we have our goals, our sense of our ideal future. As we live seeking our goals toward our perfect worlds, we encounter others. We can have a sense of 'love,' for persons who nicely fit our goals and future hopes.

For example, when I met my wife, I was training to be a minister and on break from graduate school. My obvious goal was to be a pastor, to work primarily with children and youth, to raise a family with someone who loves the church. When I met Carrie, I was working as program director for a summer camp. Intuition told me she would be a great wife, but looking back, it didn't take a reincarnation of Sherlock Holmes to figure out how she fit into my image of a perfect world. She was at camp (loves children). She was a preacher's daughter (loves church). And thought I was special (every preacher wants someone who thinks they are great).

Challenge for Us

Rather than judge others, or ourselves, as the crowd judged Zacchaeus, we should examine goals and strategies. If we understand our goals and the goals of others, we will likely understand behavior – including memories, dreams and attractions. Frustration, discouragement, and loneliness are likely the byproduct of poor goals or ineffective strategies. Sociability, self-assurance, and charity are often the result from healthy goals and effective strategies.

Reflection

Read the following quotes. How do they relate to the text and the concepts above?

When Michelangelo chiseled marble,
he could see the unfinished figure in the stone.
We are all sculptors in our behavior,
attempting to change the world outside us
to match our internal pictures of what we want.
This is true of the most simple
as well as the most complex behavior.
– Robert Wubbolding

Life can be pulled by goals just as surely as it can be pushed by drives. – Viktor Frankl

The goal of behavior is to close the gap between what the person wants and what the person perceives he or she is getting. – William Glasser

Three frogs were sitting on a log.
Two decided to jump.
How many frogs are left?
Three.
Deciding to jump means nothing.

Exercise

What is your earliest memory? What is your world view that the memory reinforces?

Think of a dream you had? What feeling did the dream stir in you? What behavior did the feeling encourage?

Zacchaeus thought that being a tax collector would give him a respected place in the community. He was mistaken. Examined goals and examines strategies are always more productive. Do you have any goals which have disappointed you?

What is a goal you have for life?
(adapted from Robert Wubbolding, *Using Reality Therapy*[ix])

Ask yourself, *"What do you want?"*
> *(If you don't know what you want, you'll never get it.)*

Evaluate your wants: Ask, "What do you really want?"
- *What would life be like if you get what you want?*
- *If you got what you want, what would you have?*
- *Is what you want attainable or realistic for you?*
- *Is there a reasonable chance of getting what you want in the near or distant future?*
- *How likely is it that the world around you will change to meet your desires?*
- *Are your wants truly in your own best interest?*
- *Would getting what you want help you? How? Would others be helped? How?*

Ask, "What are you doing?"
- *What: specific not general*
- *Are: focus on now*
- *You: personal, not external*

Evaluate behavior:
- *Is your present specific behavior helping or hurting you?*
- *Is it helping or hurting the people around you?*
- *How is it helping you get what you want?*

Ask, "What are you willing to do?"

When evaluating wants, willing action is important. Speaker Ken Davis describes meeting with his college advisor who asked him, "What do you want from life?"

Ken told him all his goals and dreams.

"I don't believe you," his advisor said.

"What do you mean?" Ken responded. "They are my dreams."

"They're your dreams alright," his advisor told him, "but I don't believe you because there is nothing in your actions that would lead me to think you're serious about them."

Your real dreams are shown through your actions – not your 'convictions.' What are you willing to do?

Jesus and the Woman at the Well
Edward Burne-Jones

There is a candle in your heart,
ready to be kindled.
There is a void in your soul,
ready to be filled.
You feel it, don't you?
Rumi

Chapter Seven: Simon, Andrew, and the Rest

Primary Concept:
We make choices based on our needs.
To understand our own behavior and the behaviors of others, we must understand the underlying need behind our choices and actions.

I have a friend who, at the end of a canoeing trip, had to get his four year old son from the canoe to a rather steep embankment. He stood in the boat, grabbed his son by the life jacket, called to a friend, "Catch." "One. Two. Three," he counted and threw his son to his friend. The friend caught the wide eyed little boy, almost. The boy slipped through his hands and slid down the embankment on his back and into the water. Dad leapt into the river turning over the canoe and retrieved his son. Now, what I can tell you, and my friend would agree, when he was standing in the boat, throwing his son to the shore made sense to him — at that time.

We make choices that make sense to us. No matter how ridiculous our choices may seem later, or at any time to an outside observer, to us, at specific places and times, often strange decisions make sense. I call it the Zacchaeus Principle. Why did Zacchaeus climb the tree? It made sense to him at that time. Why was Zacchaeus a tax collector who took money from his own people and gave it to an occupying nation while cheating his neighbors? It made sense to him at the time. I trust that Jesus saw Zacchaeus with an understanding that Zacchaeus, like all of us, did and was doing what made sense to him. Jesus understood that all Zacchaeus' behaviors had been motivated. From this perspective, unlike the community, Jesus could look at Zacchaeus and say, "So, being a tax collector, taking money from others, isn't really working for you, is it?" Jesus likely didn't even have to ask Zacchaeus how his behavior was working. Jesus could look at Zacchaeus and see the answer. Zacchaeus was up a tree.

Zacchaeus was separated from the community where he lived. You didn't have to be the Messiah or an arborist to perceive the separation between Zacchaeus and the community in which he lived.

Jesus understood that we all, like Zacchaeus, do what makes sense to us. In Luke's gospel account of the crucifixion, Jesus prays for those who are crucifying him and who sent him to be crucified, "Father forgive them, for they do not know what they are doing." They didn't understand, even though what they were doing made sense to them at the time.

The text for this chapter is Jesus' call of his followers. Read the following text. Imagine you are Simon or Andrew by the lake. Why do you think they left everything to follow Jesus? Why do you think that choice made so much sense to them at the time? Do you think they questioned their choice later?

Text

Mark 1: *As Jesus passed along the Sea of Galilee, he saw Simon and his brother Andrew casting a net into the lake—for they were fishermen. ¹⁷And Jesus said to them, 'Follow me and I will make you fish for people.'*

¹⁸And immediately they left their nets and followed him. ¹⁹As he went a little farther, he saw James son of Zebedee and his brother John, who were in their boat mending the nets.

²⁰Immediately he called them; and they left their father Zebedee in the boat with the hired men, and followed him.

Concept in the Text

The disciples had jobs. They had family businesses. At the call of Jesus, "Follow me," and the promise, "I will make you fish for people," they left family and jobs to follow him. Obviously, at the time, it made sense to them. In the call of Jesus, they heard the promise and the opportunity for something more than what they had by the Sea of Galilee. To understand them and ourselves a little better, we'll need to look at what likely motivated them, and what continually motivates us.

Concept in Depth

Abraham Maslow was another studier of human psychology that separated himself from Freud and some of Freud's foundational ideas. When Freud wanted to understand a person's behavior, he looked for a defect, because, according to Freud, defects drive our behavior. When Maslow wanted to understand a person's behavior he looked for a deficiency. For Maslow, we aren't driven by our defects, but motivated by our hungers, led by our deficits. In Maslow's needs based psychology, the key to understanding any behavior is to comprehend the lack which fuels it. Understand the need, understand the behavior.

William Glasser also studied human needs. Like Maslow, he focused not on what was wrong with a person (defect) but what was wrong with how a person was trying to get their needs met. Instead of the term, *mental health,* Glasser chose *responsible.* The responsible person responds to his or her needs in a way that gets them met and also fosters a culture or society where others can meet their needs as well.

Maslow developed a complex hierarchy of needs where lower level needs take priority over higher level needs. Glasser offered a simpler more pragmatic list of five basic needs. I have found Glasser's list easier to apply in understanding my own behaviors and the behaviors of others. According to Glasser, the five basic human needs are:

Survival: the need to keep on living.
Belonging: to be in relationship with others.
Freedom: the ability to make choices.
Power: the ability to do, to achieve, to accomplish,
Fun: to enjoy.

Applying Glasser's list of five needs to our text, why did the disciples so quickly leave family and career to follow Jesus? Perhaps they perceived in Jesus the potential to meet one or all of their needs. Consider these possibilities:

Survival. Why would the disciples leave their steady jobs as fishermen to follow Jesus? We don't know much about what it was like to be a fisherman in Jesus' day. It has been pointed out that Peter, Andrew and friends were not very good fishermen. On more than one occasion they fish all night and don't catch anything. Often, when we see them, they aren't fishing but mending their nets.

Though following Jesus doesn't sound like a guarantee for a steady meal, it may have been more promising than their jobs as fishermen.

Belonging and being loved. Jesus wasn't calling them to follow him on their own, by themselves. Jesus was not seeking a disciple, but disciples. Jesus was called them into a group where they would live together, work together, and even when sent out would go in pairs. Though they likely had a sense of belonging in their families, most people leave home at some point in their young lives looking for a greater sense of belonging than family can provide. These young men were likely no different.

Freedom. The first group of disciples were fishermen like their fathers, and likely their fathers' fathers. They chose their career from the list, "Be a fisherman like dad or be a fisherman like grandpa." Not much of a list. Jesus offered them the chance to do something different, to choose otherwise. Jesus offered freedom. In the core of Jesus' teaching is a liberation to make choices where none had been seen before. Jesus offered others the chance to accept or reject the social caste, the dictated behaviors, or assigned roles they had been given. For Jesus, love wasn't something we had to do but the greatest exercise of human freedom. For Jesus, forgiving others and loving enemies weren't dictates but liberation, empowerment, and freedom.

Power. Jesus promised them something more than being just fishermen, "I will make you fish for people," he told them. They would do something significant, meaningful, changing their world and the worlds of others. They would have an impact. They would make a difference. More than a couple of disciples saw Jesus mistakenly as an opportunity for government power and prestige. They were disappointed because Jesus had a different understanding of power, but it was power nonetheless, Godly power.

Fun. Following Jesus promised adventure. Instead of the day to day routine of fishing, every day would be different with new situations and new people.

Once we understand the needs, we understand the behaviors. Looking at the disciples through common human needs, why wouldn't they follow Jesus?

Application

One of the easiest applications of need based psychology is in working with children. The common diagnosis of defect is not nearly as effective as assessment of need. For example, when my children were very young and would fight, I didn't ask myself, "Why are my children so mean? What is wrong with them?" I asked, "What time is it?" Often with a small child the clock would do more to explain my child's behavior than any moralistic judgment. They most often fought when hungry or tired. The clock would tell me whether we needed to feed them, put them to bed, or teach them a better way to relate to their siblings.

Usually, rather than punishing a child for misbehavior, once we understand the need, we know how to help the child address it and find better, healthier strategies for meeting it. Let's look at some examples of behavior and how assessing the needs of the child might help us understand the behavior.

Example #1: Imagine a child is refusing to do his work at school. Diagnosing the defect, "You are so lazy," won't be helpful at all while assessing the deficiency may be tremendously helpful. Consider how this child's refusal to do school work can be fueled by one or more of the following needs.

Survival: Perhaps there are problems at home and the child isn't sleeping at night. If the child needs sleep, sleep will take priority over schoolwork.

Belonging: Perhaps the child's best friend is refusing to work. He wants to keep his friendship strong, so out of a need for belonging, he refuses to work like his friend.

Freedom: Perhaps he doesn't like the teacher always assigning his work and he'd like to choose, a need for freedom may be driving his behavior.

Power: Perhaps he is feeling a loss of power over a recent bad grade, in his mind, refusing to work will restore the power he feels he has lost.

Fun: Perhaps he is simply bored and wants some fun.

Example #2: Perhaps another child in the same class is making all *A's* and asking for more work. Understand her need and understand her behavior. Survival is difficult to see in this behavior, but any of the other four could be her motivators.

Belonging: Perhaps when she does well the teacher gives her praise and her friends want to study with her.

Freedom: Perhaps she get's to choose the next assignment if she scores well, and her behavior is motivated by freedom.

Power: Perhaps she gets to be line leader and work in the office if she makes good grades.

Fun: Perhaps she gets to stay out longer for recess and fun is her goal. Any or all of these needs could motivate her to score high marks.

Example #3: Listening for needs can help explain even the most puzzling behavior. My oldest daughter used to have a tremendous fear of needles. At age 10, she had to go to the doctor for a couple of shots for school. She panicked. She fought mother, nurse and doctor to the point of exhaustion (theirs, not hers). Dad was brought in. I explained to her that she would not be able to attend school in the fall without these shots. She demanded to be homeschooled. I explained that it might prevent her from getting a horrible disease and dying. She said she would rather "be diseased" than get the shot. No logical explanation or stretched rationalization had any effect. She was a bulwark, an impenetrable fortress, a fortified citadel. So, I, with all my background in human behavior and skill as parent and pastor, gave up. I came to her as a parent without all the answers. "Cayla," I said, "as your parent, I need some help. We need you to have this shot. The law dictates it. As parents we want you to be safe. Help me out, how can we get this done?" She thought for a minute and then said, "Let me get my ears pierced."

"What?" I asked.

"Let me get my ears pierced," she said again. I said nothing. She continued, "You told me that when I was ten I could have my ears pierced. I'm ten. Let me have them pierced, and I'll get the shot."

I knew it was a form of bribery. I'm not proud of it now, but those were desperate times. "Okay," I said. She went, got her shots, and we took her to get her ears pierced.

I am aware that to the outsider, the logic of a reward of needles in your ear makes no sense for a child who is terrified of needles. But, in reflection, daughter and dad have come to terms with it through understanding her need for freedom. For her, there was a great difference between the needles she chose (at the mall in her ears) and the needles she had no choice about (from the doctor in her arms). The need was freedom. The feeling was being trapped. She behaved as any animal would whether a fish on a line, a bird in a cage, or a wild horse on a rein. Facilitating her goal, the thing she was working for (her ears pierced) as part of a plan she helped create, changed, in her mind, getting a shot from oppression to choice, the act of a slave to an act of a free person which she would and did willingly endure.

Example #4: Listening for needs instead of defect is an easy way to be helpful with youth in trouble. When I get a call from a family due to a youth who has been caught smoking marijuana, I ask to meet not just with the youth or the parents, but youth and parents together. In our meeting, I follow this pattern.

First, I ask about getting caught (primarily because this is largely on their mind, and it is fun for me to hear. Usually they are pretty good stories especially if the police are involved. If there is an arrest, I can briefly tell the family what to expect which allows us to focus on more important issues.) Then I surprise youth and parents alike by asking the youth, "What did you like about smoking marijuana?"

"What?" the youth asks.

"What?" the parents repeat.

"What did you like about smoking marijuana? You must have liked it. You kept doing it."

At this point the youth looks at me and tries to judge if I'm safe or not. Most people have told him or her that smoking marijuana is bad, so they are probably wondering if I'm just setting them up to show them how wrong they were.

I ask, "What did you like?" and listen for unmet needs in their answers. Because needs motivate our behavior, smoking marijuana is then a strategy to meet several needs. Condemn the strategy before it is explored, and then you condemn the need and condemn the person. Explore why this made sense to them, you can validate the need and the person without validating the strategy.

Restating the principles: behaviors are motivated. Understand the need, understand the behavior. Applied here, smoking marijuana, like other human behaviors, is a choice that is fueled by human needs; it is, like other behaviors, a strategy. Consider how smoking marijuana may relate to the following needs:

Belonging: With marijuana, almost always, especially if they got caught, the teen is smoking with someone or a group of friends. Smoking marijuana is a group building behavior. It is something they share together. It gives them goals: score some pot, get together, and smoke it. It gives them something to talk about: "What did you feel?" "When will we get together again?" All relate to the need of belonging.

Freedom: Because smoking marijuana is illegal and against the wishes of most parents, there is a rebellion against rules, standards, and societal norms. "I can smoke it if I want to."

Power: Marijuana is smoked in secret – secret places and secret times. In secrecy is power, "I can do it, and you can't stop me."

Fun: Besides the excitement of breaking rules and not getting caught, marijuana can make boring and routine things fun. A comedy becomes funnier to the person who is high, an old video game takes on a new perspective, a disliked person becomes interesting.

The church has often focused on 'evil' desires and how to weed them out, I find it more effective to affirm God given needs. All of our needs are important, none are evil. We just choose unhealthy ways to meet those needs. While talking to the youth and family, I will affirm needs and name them in the process. Again, the needs aren't bad, the strategy is poor.

Then I ask the youth, "What did it cost you?" Usually here is where focusing on distance can help. "Are you closer to your parents now or before you started secretly smoking? What about other friends? Did you lose friends when you started smoking?" The other costs in relationship may be respect from significant adults, other family members, etc.

The parents will likely want to impress on the youth what their choice has cost them. These costs are helpful when shared in an informative, not condemning manner. Often, if the parents have had any costs in their personal history due to their own or a sibling's substance abuse, these will come out. Family secrets may be shared. I listen for ways to connect parents and youth during this time.

The discussion then goes to an affirmation of needs: belonging, power, freedom, fun, but with an attempt to find more effective strategies for meeting those needs. By focusing on needs and strategies in these situations, or in any situations of conflict, people in relationship can grow closer together through understanding.

Example #5: Through Christian history, our understanding of human behavior has been largely Freudian (though this understanding has been around long before Freud).

Like Freud, Christianity looked for defect believing that humans are motivated by our internal flaw: selfishness, evil drives, evil desires, etc. One of the best examples of our internal defect is the list of seven deadly sins cited by the early church: lust, gluttony, greed, sloth, wrath, envy, and pride. If you want to show someone what was wrong with their behavior, you just diagnosed which of the seven sins were at work.

Like Freud, Christianity has also taken a deterministic approach to human behavior. For Freud, we really make few if any choices as biology or our past determines what we will do. For the church, the doctrine of original sin states that all human behavior is shaped by sin, with little or no free choice at all. As the saying went, "The devil made me do it." The diagnosis of the church has been simple: we are evil, and because we are evil, though we may try otherwise, we will fail because it is sin living in us which determines our actions. In this approach, God is understood through how God relates not to humanity but to our sin.

There is, however, another approach. An approach that finds more help in examining the human spiritual life by looking, as we have in this chapter, at deficit rather than defect. Perhaps the most famous quote in a need based theology is from Blaise Pascal who said, "There is a God shaped vacuum in the heart of every person which cannot be filled by any created thing, but only by God, the Creator..." In this mindset, we understand that behavior is largely driven by our need for God and human suffering results when we try and fill that God shaped hole with something other than God.

Though there is not a God related need in Glasser's list, it is perhaps the central need. As Augustine said, "My heart is restless until it finds rest in Thee, O Lord." Perhaps this was the central need that led the disciples away from their nets and their families to follow after Jesus.

Challenge for Us

Jesus took a cause and effect approach to examining the behavior of others. Rather than judge their character through a dualistic good or bad diagnosis, Jesus gauged the effectiveness of their behaviors as strategies toward meeting needs. Jesus seemed to have an innate sense of the needs of others and from the awareness of their deficit, could guide them toward a healthier lifestyle which included our basic needs of: belonging, freedom, power, fun (survival never seems very high on Jesus' list of needs) and, most importantly, our spiritual need of a relationship with God.

The challenge for us is to be patient with ourselves and others. If we understand the need, we understand the behavior.

Reflection

Read the following quotes. How do they relate to the text and concepts above?

A first rate soup is better than a second rate painting. – Abraham Maslow

We cannot solve life's problems except by solving them. – Scott Peck

We need to teach the next generation of children from day one that they are responsible for their lives. – Elisabeth Kubler-Ross

Exercise

Look at the following list of behaviors. What needs are likely motivating the behavior? Can you think of a better strategy to meeting the needs than the one listed?

Behavior	Needs	Different Strategy
Spending large amounts of money on lottery tickets		
A youth joins a gang		
Driving fast		
Having an affair		
Watching television all weekend		
Smoking		
Eating ice cream sundaes after fighting with spouse		

Do you have any defective strategies in your life that need to be examined?

Adoration of the Magi
Andrea Mantegna 1460

The cave you fear to enter
holds the treasure you seek.
Joseph Campbell

Chapter Eight: Herod

Primary Concept:
*People and events don't bother us.
Our perceptions of them do.*

Come with me to our local assisted living facility. We walk into the apartment of church member number one. She sits in her wheel chair, and you and I sit beside her in a couple of high back chairs. We ask about the home. "It's a good place to live," member number one tells us. "The food is okay. It is actually a little bit better since they hired a new cook. I like the staff; they are very nice to me. I'd rather be back at my house, but if I can't be there, this is as good a place as any."

We leave church member number one and go down the hall and around the corner to the apartment of church member number two. She sits in her wheel chair, and you and I sit beside her in a couple of high back chairs. We ask about the home. "I hate it," she says. "It is a terrible place to live. The food is terrible. It is almost always cold. They serve breakfast too early. The staff members are too rough and are always mean to me."

Now, both women live in the same building, on the same hall, with the same food, the same staff. It is not the home that is different for each; it is their perceptions of it. We don't live in the world, we live in our image of the world. We don't relate to others, we relate to our images of others. We don't react to life, we react to our perceptions of life.

Read the following story of Herod "The Great" (who ruled at the time Jesus was born, not Herod Anitpas referred to later in the gospels). Note how he relates not to Jesus but to his perception of Jesus.

Text

Text: Matthew 1: *In the time of King Herod, after Jesus was born in Bethlehem of Judea, wise men from the East came to Jerusalem,* ² *asking, "Where is the child who has been born king of the Jews? For we observed his star at its rising, and have come to pay him homage." ³ When King Herod heard this, he was frightened, and all Jerusalem with him;*

And then later, when the Magi had chosen to go home by another way, *¹⁶ When Herod saw that he had been tricked by the wise men, he was infuriated, and he sent and killed all the children in and around Bethlehem who were two years old or under, according to the time that he had learned from the wise men.*

Concept in the Text

Herod's encounter with Jesus is different from all other encounters listed in this book. Unlike the rest, Herod never met Jesus. Herod never saw Jesus. Herod was never in the same room or the same town as Jesus, and was only in the same country as Jesus for the first two years of Jesus' life. Yet, without any contact, Herod has the most intense reaction to Jesus of anyone. With the simple news of Jesus' birth, unlike the Magi who were excited about the possibility and searched for the newborn king, Herod became so anxious that he had all the children under the age of two in Bethlehem killed.

Clearly, Herod wasn't reacting to Jesus the person but Jesus the idea. It was not the magi, their message, or the newborn Jesus who scared Herod. Herod was frightened by his perception of Jesus, by the image of Jesus he had in his mind. We know that Jesus would actually play no threat to Herod or his position. Jesus would soon leave the country and Herod would be dead before Jesus returned.

To understand Herod's choice, and how his horrifying actions might have made sense to anyone, we need a clearer understanding of how Herod imagined Jesus. Herod had several key assumptions when he heard of Jesus' birth which led to his anxious response:

My place in the world is centered on my role as king.

My life is better when I am king than it would be if I'm not.

There can be only one king. There is not room for another. If another king arises, I would lose my place. Life as I know it would end.

Kings tend to kill other rulers who may be a threat. Kings are easier to kill as babies than as adults. If there is a newborn king, I must have him killed as soon as possible in order to stay safe.

Herod's idea of Jesus didn't fit into his idea of himself (as king) or his understanding of the world (there can be only one king of this region – me!). Lost in his thoughts and building on all the assumptions listed above, having all the babies in Bethlehem under the age of two killed in order to get to Jesus made a lot of sense to Herod.

Concept in Depth

Like Herod, we live our lives relating primarily to our perceptions of people and situations. That's how our minds work. In the words of Alfred Adler,

Human beings live in the realm of meanings. We do not experience things in the abstract; we always experience them in human terms. Even at its source our experience is qualified by our human perspective. 'Wood' means 'wood in its relation to humankind', and 'stone' means 'stone as a factor in human life'. Anyone who tried to consider circumstances, to the exclusion of meanings, would be very unfortunate: he would isolate himself from others and his actions would be useless to himself or to anyone else; in a word, they would be meaningless. But no human being can escape meanings. We experience reality only through the meaning we ascribe to it: not as a thing in itself, but as something interpreted. It is natural to conclude, therefore, that this meaning is always more or less unfinished, or incomplete, and even that it can never be altogether right. The realm of meanings is thus the realm of mistakes.

Adler wasn't questioning God, truth, or reality, but simply our perceptions of them. A student of Adler, Rudolf Dreikurs commented that *(People) are good observers, just lousy interpreters.*

Years after Adler, Albert Ellis, with a similar basis on human perceptions, developed Rational Emotive Therapy. Instead of looking at what is wrong with us (Freud), Ellis asked "What's wrong with our thinking?" Ellis believed that it is thinking which leads to action, so dysfunctional thinking will lead to unhealthy actions. Ellis summed up his theory by quoting the first century philosopher Epictetus, *Men are disturbed not by things, but by the views which they take of them.* For Ellis, events don't make us 'feel good' or 'feel bad'. We do it to ourselves with the thoughts we choose. For Ellis, thoughts, feelings and behavior are all related.

If you want to change how you feel about an event or a person, change how you think about them.[2]

To examine our thoughts, behaviors, and feelings, Rational-Emotive Therapy offers a helpful tool:

The ABC'S of Behavior.

A = Activating Event or Circumstance: What happened.
B = Belief System: What I was thinking.
C = Consequence (Emotional): What I felt.
C = Consequence (Behavioral): What I did. [x]

Applying the ABC's of Behavior to Herod, we see how his thinking influenced his feeling (anxiety) and behavior (killing children).
A =Activating Event or Circumstance: What happened. *Magi from the East came and told me of a new star which is a sign of a new born king.*
B = Belief System: What I was thinking. *A new king would be a threat. I could lose everything.*
C = Consequence (Emotional): What I felt. *Afraid.*
C = Consequence (Behavioral): What I did. *I sought to assure my place in the world by killing the newborn king. To make sure he was dead, I had all males less than two years of age put to death.*

Had Herod interpreted the announcement of the new king differently then Herod would have felt and acted differently. If Herod had interpreted the news of the new born king by thinking, *The new king is the promised Messiah; He will teach us a new way to live and bring a kingdom of peace,* then he might have gone with the magi. His goal clearly would have been safety for children of Bethlehem and not death. Herod had a choice – he could see Jesus as an opportunity or a threat. By choosing to see Jesus as a threat, his emotions and reactions followed.

Application

The ABC's of Behavior works well for not only examining kings, but the rest of us as well. Robert L. Leahy in *Cognitive Therapy Techniques* offers the following chart to illustrate how thinking affects our feelings and our behaviors in response to everyday situations.[xi] The first two rows are answered for you.

A = Activating Event	B = Belief (Thought)	C = Consequence: Feelings	C = Consequence: Behaviors
I hear the window rattling.	Someone is breaking into my house.	Anxious	Lock the door, call police.
I hear the window rattling.	It's windy outside and the window is old and loose.	Slightly irritated	Try to tighten the window, go back to sleep.
A man is approaching me on a dark, empty street.	I'm going to get mugged.		
A man is approaching me on a dark, empty street.	I wonder if that's my old friend Steve.		
My husband is sitting reading the newspaper.	He doesn't care about my feelings.		
My husband is sitting reading the newspaper.	He's withdrawing from me because he's angry with me.		.
I feel my heart beating rapidly.	I'm having a heart attack.		
I feel my heart beating rapidly.	I've had too much coffee.		

Similar to Herod, the above situations can all be divided into two perceptions (threat or opportunity.) Like Herod, we have the choice in every situation to see opportunity or threat. We can rest assured that it is never the threat itself that bothers us; it is our perception of it.

Challenge for Us

On several occasions in the gospels, Jesus asks, "What do you think?" And that's where he starts. Before we examine what's wrong with the world, the first place to look is our own thinking. Jesus would have us consider how we think about God, others, the world, our own problems and consider how our actions are shaped by what we think. Are we living healthy productive lives in lasting relationships? If not, what's wrong with our thinking?

Reflection

Read the story and the following quotes. How do you see them exhibited in the above story of Herod and in the theory of Albert Ellis?

Experience is not what happens to a man. It is what a man does with what happens to him. – Aldous Huxley

Our life always expresses the result of our dominant thoughts. – Soren Kierkegaard

Men are disturbed not by things, but by the views which they take of them. – Epictetus

Conflict often comes when members fail to see each other as separate human beings but as abstractions: powerful entities, threatening forces, wild images. Caught in a storm of anger, each is a threat to the power of the other, not a person. – Carl Whitaker

Exercise

Describe a situation about which you felt afraid.

A = Activating event. What happened that triggered your fear?

B = Beliefs. What did you think at the time?

C = Consequences (Emotional): How did you feel? How were your feelings a product of your thinking?

C = Consequences (Behavioral): What did you do?

D = Dispute. How would you have felt and acted differently if you had interpreted the situation differently?

Jesus
Gustave Dore

The mind is its own place, and in itself
can make a Heav'n of Hell, a Hell of Heav'n.
Milton

Chapter Nine: Amos

Primary Concept:
We set the distance
between ourselves and others
based on safety.

We move in relationship with others. There are only two movements: toward others and away from others. Movements result from one of two goals, to be closer or to have space. When we want to be closer, we often move toward others. And, when we want space, we often move away. However, we also reverse the behavior. We often move toward others when we want distance, like an angry dog barking that moves closer to you so that you will go away. We also move away from others when we want to be closer, like a baby who has climbed out of bed, walks into the living room naked, and says, "Chase me." The baby moves away from you but clearly wants you to catch her.

Ironically, though we constantly move toward others and away, though we chase and we flee, the distances between us and significant others in our lives are usually kept relatively constant. Largely unaware, with others, we agree upon the emotional distance between us and work together to maintain that distance over the life of the relationship.

Read the following passage. Where do you see movement toward others or away? What actions are intended to get others to move? What actions are intended to maintain already established distances?

Text

Mark 5: *(Jesus and the disciples) came to the other side of the sea, to the country of the Gerasenes. 2 And when (Jesus) had stepped out of the boat, immediately a man out of the tombs with an unclean spirit met him. 3 He lived among the tombs; and no one could restrain him any more, even with a chain; 4 for he had often been restrained with shackles and chains, but the chains he wrenched apart, and the shackles he broke in pieces; and no one had the* strength to subdue him. ⁵ Night and day among the tombs and on the mountains he was always howling and bruising himself with stones.

⁶ When he saw Jesus from a distance, he ran and bowed down before him; ⁷ and he shouted at the top of his voice, "What have you to do with me, Jesus, Son of the Most High God? I adjure you by God, do not torment me." ⁸ For he had said to him, "Come out of the man, you unclean spirit!"

⁹ Then Jesus asked him, "What is your name?" He replied, "My name is Legion; for we are many." ¹⁰ He begged him earnestly not to send them out of the country.

¹¹ Now there on the hillside a great herd of swine was feeding; ¹² and the unclean spirits begged him, "Send us into the swine; let us enter them."

¹³ So he gave them permission. And the unclean spirits came out and entered the swine; and the herd, numbering about two thousand, rushed down the steep bank into the sea, and were drowned in the sea.

¹⁴ The swineherds ran off and told it in the city and in the country. Then people came to see what it was that had happened. ¹⁵ They came to Jesus and saw the demoniac sitting there, clothed and in his right mind, the very man who had had the legion; and they were afraid. ¹⁶ Those who had seen what had happened to the demoniac and to the swine reported it. ¹⁷ Then they began to beg Jesus to leave their neighborhood.

¹⁸ As he was getting into the boat, the man who had been possessed by demons begged him that he might be with him.

¹⁹ But Jesus refused, and said to him, "Go home to your friends, and tell them how much the Lord has done for you, and what mercy he has shown you." ²⁰ And he went away and began to proclaim in the Decapolis how much Jesus had done for him; and everyone was amazed.

Concept in the Text

The gospel writer doesn't tell us this man's name. To treat him as a person and not as an illness, I am going to refer to the man with unclean spirits as Amos. 'Amos' means 'burdened'. The man obviously had some burdens.

Answering "Who am I?" and "What's wrong with me?" for Amos is not complicated. The town diagnosed him quickly, "Who is he?" "He is evil!" they cried. "What's wrong with him?" "He is possessed by demons!" From their diagnosis, they prescribed, "The best thing to do is lock him up!" So they did. Their diagnosis, like ours, was easy, though not very helpful. More helpful are the questions "Where is he?" and "Where is he moving?"

Where was he? He was living away from everyone else. He had been locked up, restrained with shackles and chains, distant, controlled, separated from and by the town.

Where was he moving? Amos didn't stay locked up. He broke free. Yet, freed from captivity, he didn't move toward town but away. The town was afraid of Amos, and Amos was afraid of the town, too. To keep themselves safe from Amos, they locked him up. To keep himself safe from the town he went to the mountains, or if he came nearer to town, he stayed in the tombs. The town kept distance from Amos by locking him up, and he kept distance from the town by living in a graveyard and acting scary.

Then Jesus moved toward Amos and the town. Amos tried to get Jesus to go away by running toward him and yelling. For the purpose of this chapter, I'm not going to try and explain demons or what Jesus' does with them. I have no rational explanation, and even if I did, there have been enough commentaries on this aspect of the passage. There have been few serious examinations of the movements and the motivations. Amos moved toward Jesus like a violent bear. Jesus didn't react. Amos strategy didn't work because Jesus didn't go away. Jesus chose his own distance apart from Amos' actions. Jesus chose to move toward him. Jesus had no anxiety so Amos had no power over him. For Amos, a new distance had to be negotiated. He saw he couldn't control Jesus through yelling and so he gave up the strategy. He asked Jesus for mercy. Unlike the people from the town, Jesus doesn't move away or send Amos away, just his demons. They have no power at setting distance. Jesus does.

What Amos was afraid of happened – someone moved closer to him. Though earlier, he may have felt that if anyone got close enough to him he would surely die, he didn't die. He was then, as described by the text, "in his right mind," calm, at peace.

111

Though Amos was now composed, the anxiety didn't seem to go with the demons into the pigs, but instead, it was magnified in the town's people. They were afraid. They had been comfortable with Amos like he was before when they knew what to do with him, when they felt he was under control. Amos was in his right mind, the town wasn't. They were afraid, if Amos moved back toward town, how could they ever feel safe? What if he went nuts again? To be safe, they were sure they had to distance themselves from Amos and even more from Jesus. Jesus obviously didn't respect the space they valued as essential to their peace of mind. The distance they worked so hard to maintain meant nothing to Jesus. In moving toward the town's resident lunatic, Jesus moved toward them and overstepped their protective boundary. As they had with Amos, they wanted to feel safe from Jesus, who was in many ways more frightening than Amos because he was not a respecter of their established borders. To feel safe, in an attempt to calm their anxiety, they asked Jesus to leave.

As Jesus started to go, Amos' new confidence wavered. "Take me with you," he asked Jesus. Amos was still afraid of the town's people. He still wanted distance from them, though instead of living in the tombs, he had a different strategy, going away with Jesus.

"Go home to your friends," Jesus instructed him. As Jesus defused the first strategy, the fight mentality in which Amos had used his demons' violence to maintain distance, so too does he defuse the new strategy, the flight attempt of leaving with Jesus. To every reader's surprise, Jesus called the town's people Amos' 'friends.' Could Jesus be referring to those people who locked Amos up as his 'friends?' Jesus doesn't diagnose the town's people as evil any more than he diagnosed Amos as evil. He does diagnose and attempt to treat their distance problem. Amos and the people from town were more alike than they recognized. They both suffered from distance problems; they both were possessed by their fear of each other; they both acted in ways to calm their fears and maintain distance. Jesus wanted Amos to stay as his representative, and, as peacefully as Jesus had moved toward Amos, so did Jesus want Amos to peacefully move toward the anxiety-ridden town's people. The hope for Amos and for the town Jesus left with Amos and his new found ability to move toward others in a way that decreased, not increased, distance.

112

Concept in Depth

Amos was diagnosed as being possessed by demons. Today, he likely would be diagnosed as being schizophrenic. Family Systems Theory began after psychologists started looking at the treatment plan of people diagnosed with schizophrenia. While hospitalized in treatment, they got better. When they went back home the symptoms returned. The question was raised by these theorists as to how the symptoms functioned within the family unit as a whole for clearly they did not exist in the same way outside of the family relationships. The schizophrenia served a purpose within the family. Adler addressed the use of symptoms when he said, *We must never neglect the patient's own use of his symptoms.* Amos had symptoms, lots of them, and he used them.

Examining functions of symptoms is aided by looking at distances between people. Consider this example by Alder.

A boy at one school, the laziest boy in the class, was asked by his teacher, 'Why do you do so badly in your schoolwork?' He answered, 'If I am the laziest boy here, you will always give me lots of your time. You never pay any attention to good boys, who never disturb the class and do all their work properly.' So long as his aim was to attract attention and to control his teacher, he had found the best way to do it. It would be no use trying to get rid of his laziness: he needed his laziness for his goal. From this point of view he was perfectly in the right, and if he changed his behavior he would be a fool.

Parents and teachers alike had probably diagnosed his character deficiency as lazy, undisciplined, slothful, and insolent. "Who am I?" helped little. Looking at distance and his goal of getting his teacher to move closer, we understand his behavior. Understand the goal, understand the behavior. He liked being close to his teacher, he liked her attention. By not doing his work, she stayed close to him (at least until she heard the disclosure above).

Distance between people is not decided by one person, but negotiated back and forth between people. Once the teacher knows his goal, she likely did not move toward him in the same way when he wasn't doing his work. Together they probably reached a new agreed upon distance.

In the passage above, Amos and the town agreed upon the distance between them. The town didn't exile Amos alone; Amos and the town both accepted his place in the name of safety – the town from Amos and Amos from the town. Intimacy isn't the goal of most relationships, stability is. Growth isn't the goal of most of our movements, safety is. In relationships that have achieved an agreed upon balance, change is seldom welcomed because change is often a threat to stability, safety, consistency and balance.

Consider the following couple: The husband in the family stops drinking. Sober, he starts paying more attention to his wife, children and their home. He also starts observing some things around the house, and in the family members, that need improvement. He had improved and wanted mother and children to join on his personal growth crusade. At the end of two weeks, he has cleaned and painted the laundry room, joined the Y, and made two A.A. meetings a day for two weeks. To celebrate his getting his two week chip at A.A., his wife throws a dinner party with close friends. She buys a bottle of wine to celebrate. At dinner, the visiting couple and the wife have wine; he has soda water. They all say how proud they are of him. The bottle she bought was quite large. There is a lot left over. That night, after the party, husband and wife have a fight. She goes to bed. He stays up with the bottle. He begins drinking again. Obviously, his new movement toward his spouse and the children was not well received. It challenged the stability of their agreed upon distance. By enabling his drinking, the distance between them is restored to its prior place.

When examined, we see how we often sabotage our own intimacy with others by maintaining 'safe' distances. Jesus goal was never safety. His goal is intimacy, real relationships not marred by false distances, which is why his common instruction is "Go." Again and again throughout the gospels, Jesus sends people, "Go." Jesus is never content with our false barriers of separation. "Go." It's no wonder. The God of the Bible not only moves, God sends: Abram and Sarai to a new land, Joseph to Egpyt, Moses to Egypt, Israel to the Promised Land, all the prophets are sent to speak truth to power, again and again God sends. Jesus sees not only the movement of God but the sending of God. Jesus says in John, "As the Father has sent me, so I send you." The last thing he does in the gospel of Matthew

(28) is send the disciples, "Go into all the world."

Amos wants to go with Jesus. Amos wants to maintain his distance from the town. In the Hebrew Scriptures, the prophet Amos was a reluctant prophet. God sent him, but he didn't want to go. He preferred staying distant, safe. In a similar manner, when Amos complains here, when he wants to go where it is safer, with Jesus (or so he thinks), Jesus won't hear of it. "Go home..."

Challenge for Us

Intimacy involves risk. If we are brave enough to risk the vulnerability of intimacy, we may have fuller and more rewarding relationships. To grow closer, distances must change. Someone must move.

Reflection

In my early professional years I was asking the question: How can I treat, or cure, or change this person? Now I would phrase the question in this way: How can I provide a relationship which this person may use for his own personal growth? – Carl Amoss

The good life is a process, not a state of being. It is a direction not a destination. – Carl Amoss

Love does not alter the beloved, it alters itself. – Soren Kierkegaard

We live in a world of things, and our only connection with them is that we know how to manipulate or to consume them. – Erich Fromm

The art of love is largely the art of persistence. – Albert Ellis

Whenever we give our hearts in love, the burden of our vulnerability grows. We risk being rebuffed or embarrassed or inadequate. Beyond these things, we risk the enormous pain of loss... If we insulate our hearts from suffering, we shall only subdue the very thing that makes life worth living. We cannot protect

ourselves from loss. We can only protect ourselves from the death of love, we are left only with the aching hollow of regret, that haunting emptiness where love might have been.
— Forrest Church

Exercise

Amos, in the scripture passage, used his symptoms to keep a consistent distance.

Do you have any symptoms which you use to manage distance in your relationships?

How do you move when you feel angry? Afraid? Comfortable? Safe?

Judas
Fyodor Bronnikov

One can choose to go back toward safety or forward toward growth. Growth must be chosen again and again; fear must be overcome again and again.–
Abraham Maslow

Chapter Ten: Judas

Primary Concept:
No matter how others relate to us,
we can always choose our response.

I went to orientation for my first day of school. Returning from the bathroom toward my soon to be classroom, I was happy. I was proud to be a first grader. I bounced down the hall, and whistled on my way. A giant (at least to me) of a man approached. He looked down on me in a voice as deep as the bottom of the sea, "We don't whistle at school." Like a puppy with tail tucked behind me, I slowly and quietly walked back to my class.

I learned more about the principal later on. All students were told, "If you misbehave (which was don't do what the teacher tells you or do what the teacher tells you not to), you will be sent to the corner. If you continue to misbehave, you'll have to stand out in the hall. If you continue to misbehave you'll get sent to the office to see the principal." And later we learned what happened when you went to the principal's office. "He called my parents," one child said. "I got paddled," offered another. Who was the principal for me at age six? The giant with the paddle. Why didn't you misbehave? Because you didn't want to go to the principal's office.

Even now, some thirty-five plus years later, when I go to an elementary school and walk down the hall, I have a great temptation to whistle but don't because I hear the gruff voice of a Goliath say, "We don't whistle in school."

William Glasser defined psychology as *the way we approach others.* The most popular psychology, according to Glasser, is this: *punish the people who are doing wrong, so they will do what we say is right; then reward them, so they keep doing what we want them to do.* He calls this approach *External Control Psychology.*[xii]

Read the following passage. Consider, how does Judas and the crowd approach Jesus? How do you see control psychology in the actions of the crowd? In the unnamed disciple?

Text

Matthew 26: *47 While (Jesus) was still speaking, Judas, one of the twelve, arrived; with him was a large crowd with swords and clubs, from the chief priests and the elders of the people. 48 Now the betrayer had given them a sign, saying, "The one I will kiss is the man; arrest him."*

49 At once he came up to Jesus and said, "Greetings, Rabbi!" and kissed him.

50 Jesus said to him, "Friend, do what you are here to do." Then they came and laid hands on Jesus and arrested him.

51 Suddenly, one of those with Jesus put his hand on his sword, drew it, and struck the slave of the high priest, cutting off his ear.

52 Then Jesus said to him, "Put your sword back into its place; for all who take the sword will perish by the sword. 53 Do you think that I cannot appeal to my Father, and he will at once send me more than twelve legions of angels? 54 But how then would the scriptures be fulfilled, which say it must happen in this way?"

55 At that hour Jesus said to the crowds, "Have you come out with swords and clubs to arrest me as though I were a bandit? Day after day I sat in the temple teaching, and you did not arrest me. 56 But all this has taken place, so that the scriptures of the prophets may be fulfilled."

Then all the disciples deserted him and fled.

Concept in the Text

In this passage is a distinct contrast between one open hand surrounded by many closed hands.

The crowd moved toward Jesus with closed hands. They carried swords and clubs. No one can carry a sword or club with an open hand; it would fall to the ground. Those who grabbed Jesus closed their hands upon him. Peter (according to John 18:10) grabbed a sword with a closed hand. Symbolically, the Pharisees may be thought of as shaking a fist at Jesus. Angry people shake fists. The disciples who fled had closed fists as they ran away. In fear, we run with closed hands, not open.

Jesus, on the other hand, did not strike with the sword; he did not shake his fist in anger; he did not run with a closed hand. He stayed open to others, specifically to Judas. He called Judas 'friend.' "Friend, do what you are here to do."

When Peter struck someone, Jesus replied, "Put your sword back into its place; for all who take the sword will perish by the sword. Do you think that I cannot appeal to my Father, and he will at once send me more than twelve legions of angels?" In other words, "If I wanted closed hands, I wouldn't need yours. I could have an army of angels." Open hand verses closed hands.

For Jesus, the open hand is clearly a conscious choice. For everyone else, the closed hand is less of a conscious choice and more of a reaction. Consider how Peter grabbed his sword after the crowd, prepared to take Jesus away, grabbed Jesus. Matthew says, "Suddenly..." 'Suddenly' is a reactive word. He reacted to their action. If you would have asked him later about grabbing the sword, Peter, who earlier had vowed to die with Jesus before he would deny him, Peter, who couldn't imagine ever abandoning Jesus though others might run away, Peter, in disbelief of his own behavior, would likely have placed blame outside of his own power to choose, "I didn't have any choice. They grabbed Jesus. They came with spears. They made me fight..."

Robert Fritz in his book, *The Path of Least Resistance,* points out two approaches to life: acting and reacting. He gives characteristics of reactive people: They *believe that circumstances are the driving force of life, are generally cynical, have a short fuse, react suddenly, hold conspiracy theories about people in power, subscribe to a religious philosophy that reacts against injustice or evil, see themselves in life situations they must overcome to survive, contain a basic presumption that they are powerless in the world, that power is always outside them, not within them.*

Jesus, in contrast, was not cynical, did not have a short fuse, did not hold conspiracy theories, was not different in differing situations, did not see power as something outside himself but within. He did not blame anyone. He did not react. Jesus acted. Jesus chose.

Concept in Depth

Ivan Pavlov had a great impact on psychology. Remember Pavlov's dog experiment (1890)? Pavlov observed that every time he brought out food for his dog, the dog would salivate. He then started a process with his dog called conditioning. He rang a bell every time he brought out the food. Over time, he kept ringing the bell every time he brought food. Then he found that the dog would salivate every time he rang the bell whether he brought the food or not. He had conditioned the dog to associate the sound of the bell with food and to salivate when he heard the bell. Through the stimulus connected with the food, Pavlov controlled the dog's behavior.

Behavioral psychology has the theory that, like dogs, people can be conditioned to give desired responses if we can use the right stimulus. We see this mentality in advertising (What stimulus can I use to get you to buy my product?), politics (What can I say to get you to vote for me?) and in schools, work environments, and homes (What reward or punishment can I use to get you to do what I want?). Behaviorist B.F. Skinner said, "Give me a child, and I'll shape him into anything."

William Glasser terms this approach to others as *External Control Psychology.*[xiii]

Control psychology assumes:

- Others can control me including how I feel and what I do.
- I can control others if I can find the right stimuli, motivation, or reward.
- I know better than others what is right/just and what is better for others including what they want, need, and should do.
- I am right and just in rewarding those who do well and punishing those who do poorly.

In Judas, Peter, the crowd and the Pharisees, we see control psychology in action. Judas used the Pharisees as stimulus to try and control Jesus' behavior. The Pharisees used soldiers as stimulus to try and control Jesus and all his followers.

Peter used a sword to try and control the soldiers by attacking one of them. Even though it is the most common approach to others, Control Psychology is not a very effective way to live.

Alphie Kohn cites a list of parenting books which are obviously about gaining control over children. The list includes, *Don't be afraid to Discipline: Parents in Charge: Parents in Control; Taking Charge: Back in Control: Disciplining Your Preschooler – and Feeling Good About It, 'Cause I'm the Mommy, That's Why.*[xiv] Kohn, in lecture and print, points out that a Pavlovian approach to people would be effective if people were like dogs. Kohn asserts that we are not like dogs at all, but more like cats.

Have you ever called a cat? "Here kitty, kitty." A cat will come, but only if it wants to. Call a cat, he may look at you. "What? Get up? I'm not coming over there." Cats seldom react to human attempts to condition their behavior. As the saying goes, "You can get a cat to go wherever you want, but only if the cat wants to." If you are a parent, is your child more cat-like or dog-like in behavior? Do they come when you call? I tell prospective parents, "If you want an animal to come when you call, don't have a child, get a dog." People aren't like dogs. People are like cats. Control Psychologies are no more effective with people than with cats.

Jesus, in stark contrast to others in the text, didn't try and control anyone nor was anyone able to control Jesus. He approached those in the text who came for him with the same psychology he had approached others with all along, psychology which William Glasser calls "Choice Psychology." Glasser points out that our life is governed not by outside forces, but by our choices. Glasser often asks. When the phone rings, what do you do? Answer it. Why? Because the phone rang? No, you answer it because you choose to. When you approach an intersection, what do you do? Stop. Why? The light is red? No, you stop because you choose to. There is always choice. We always have choice.

In contrast to Control Psychology, Choice Psychology assumes:[xv]

- Others can't control me unless I give them control. I always have a choice unless I give my choice away.
- Though I may try, I can't control others effectively.
- I don't know what is best for others. All I can give is information.
- Neither punishments nor rewards are effective ways of relating.

In the text, Jesus did not resist Judas, "Friend, do what you're here to do." Jesus was clear that even though they were making choices to control him, he would not react to them. He would not give up his power to continue making his own choices. He responded to them, but he did not react. Peter reacted. Unlike Peter, Jesus affirmed he had made his choice and wasn't choosing violence. He said to Peter in essence, "Put away your sword, if I wanted control, I would call an army of angels." Jesus neither controlled others nor did he let others take his power to choose.

Application

When Jesus called disciples, he didn't call them to give up their power to choose – but to claim it. Nowhere is this power more evident than in Jesus' call to forgive and in his call to love our enemies. Only in Choice Psychology do we understand loving our enemies as empowerment. With a Control Psychology, loving enemies is only done out of obedience to a higher authority – we love enemies, we forgive others because someone: Jesus, the preacher, or our mother, said we should. In Choice Psychology we love enemies because we choose to, not because we are commanded to, but on the contrary, we are liberated by Jesus and can choose it. To love your enemies is the greatest power of all.

I saw this power when I was seven years old. I saw this power in an enemy, Greg Chambers. Greg was actually my best friend. He had come over to my house to play. For some reason, I don't remember why, I got mad at Greg. Furious, I was chasing him around the house.

"I'm going to kill you, Greg!" I yelled.

"No you're not," he said as he ran away.

"Yes I am," I screamed.

"No you're not," he replied.

"How do you know?" I asked.

"Because I said so," was his response.

The more I chased him the madder I got and the calmer he became. His 'because I said so' infuriated me. He was right. There was no way I was going to kill him. I couldn't catch him. He was a lot faster than I was. So, instead of threatening his life, I threatened our friendship.

"You are not my best friend."

"Yes I am," he replied, still out running me.

"No you're not."

"Yes I am."

"Why?"

"Because I said so."

At the arrest, Jesus called Judas, "Friend," not because he had to but because he chose to. Jesus on the cross prayed, "Father forgive them because they don't know what they are doing." Forgiveness was power – not because he had to – but because he could – he chose to and calls us to do the same.

The famous prayer of St. Francis is all about choice. Though the word 'choose' is not in the original, it is implied.

Lord, make me an instrument of Thy peace;
where there is hatred, let me CHOOSE *love;*
where there is injury, let me CHOOSE *pardon;*
where there is doubt, let me CHOOSE *faith;*
where there is despair, let me CHOOSE *hope;*
where there is darkness, let me CHOOSE *light;*
and where there is sadness, let me CHOOSE *joy.*

The open hand is not a commandment – but the choice of free people, of liberated people, of Jesus people. This power of choice, evident in the passage, is a far greater power than frightened, reacting, closed fisted people understand.

There are many more people beside Jesus who have understood the power of choice, who chose that power even in terrifying and tragic circumstances. One of the best examples I discovered was in the choices of Bishop Hassam Dehqani Tafti. He was the first Iranian to become an Anglican bishop. He was the bishop of the Episcopal Church in the Middle East. He lived constantly threatened by fundamentalist Islamists. They burst into his bedroom one night, fired four shots into his pillow, barely missing his head, wounding his wife. Later, his secretary was tied up and shot. While attending a meeting in Cyprus he received a phone call from England that his son had been shot and killed. He had all the choices of Jesus – do I approach the world with an open hand or a closed fist? Do I approach those who consider themselves my enemies and want to hurt and kill me with love or hate? Do I respond or react? And, like Jesus, he chose the open hand over the closed fist; he chose love over hate; he chose to respond rather than react.

This is how he responded to his son's murder. He wrote this prayer the day before his son's funeral titled, 'A father's prayer upon the murder of his son:'

O God,

We remember not only Bahram (our son), but also his murderers;
Not because they killed him in the prime of his youth
and made our hearts bleed and our tears flow,
Not because with this savage act
they have brought further disgrace
on the name of our country
among the civilized nations of the world;
But because of their crime
we now follow thy footsteps more closely
in the way of sacrifice.
The terrible fire of this calamity
burns up all selfishness and possessiveness in us;
Its flame reveals the depths of
depravity and meanness and suspicion,
the dimension of hatred and
the measure of sinfulness in human nature;
It makes obvious as never before
our need to trust in God's love as shown
in the cross of Jesus and his resurrection;
Love which makes us free of hate towards our persecutors;
Love which brings patience, forbearance, courage,
loyalty, humility, generosity, greatness of heart;
Love which more than ever deepens our trust
in God's final victory and his eternal designs
for the church and for the world;
Love which teaches us how to prepare
to face our own day of death.
O God, Bahram's blood (our son's blood)
has multiplied the fruit of the Spirit in the soil of our souls;
So when his murderers stand before Thee on the day of judgment
remember the fruit of the Spirit
by which they have enriched our lives.
And forgive.[xvi]

Challenge for Us

Even in confrontational and conflicted situations, we can always choose who we will be, how we will act, and what we will do if we are only brave enough to claim our power to choose.

Reflection

The quotes are from Viktor Frankl who developed his psychology in a concentration camp during World War II. How do they apply to the text and the concepts above?

The one thing you can't take away from me is the way I choose to respond to what you do to me. – Frankl

Between stimulus and response there is a space. In that space is our power to choose our response. In our response lies our growth and our freedom. – Frankl

Each man is questioned by life; and he can only answer to life by answering for his own life; to life he can only respond by being responsible. – Frankl

Exercise

Fill in the following statements: (External)[xvii]

1. I had to _ _____ , _____, ___.
2. I can't _____, _, _____ .
3. I need __ _____ , _____, _____.
4. I'm afraid to _____ , _____ , _____ ___.
5. I'm unable to , _____ , _____ .

Now, go back and try substituting these words for the five beginnings above: (Internal)

1. "I chose to" instead of "I had to."
2. "I won't" instead of "I can't."
3. "I want" instead of "I need."
4. "I'd like to" instead of "I'm afraid to."
5. "I'm unwilling to work hard enough to" instead of "I'm unable to."

Read through St. Francis' prayer and answer the following:
Lord, make us instruments of Thy peace;
where there is hatred, let me CHOOSE love;
Where do you need to choose love over hate in my life?

where there is injury, let me CHOOSE pardon;
Where do you need to choose pardon over injury?

where there is doubt, let me CHOOSE faith;
Where do you need to choose faith over doubt?

where there is despair, let me CHOOSE hope;
Where do you need to choose hope over despair?

where there is darkness, let me CHOOSE light;
Where do you need to choose light over darkness?

and where there is sadness, let me CHOOSE joy.
Where do you need to choose joy over sadness?

Hands from *Creation of Adam*
Michelangelo Buonarroti 1512

Life cannot be understood flat on a page. It has to be lived; a person has to get out of his head, has to fall in love, has to memorize poems, has to jump off bridges into rivers, has to stand in an empty desert and whisper sonnets under his breath... We get one story, you and I, and one story alone. God has established the elements, the setting and the climax and resolution. It would be a crime not to venture out, wouldn't it?
Donald Miller

Chapter Eleven: Amy

**Primary Concept:
We can always claim our place in the world.
We can choose to accept or reject
where others try to place us.**

Remember 'cooties?' Cooties is that game in elementary school, where someone declares that one kid in the class has 'cooties.' If that child touches you or you touch that child or that child's stuff, then you become cootified. You have cooties, your stuff has cooties, and your mama has cooties. That's the way cooties works.

The only difference for the woman in this text and 'cooties' in the elementary school, was that for her, rejection was no game and segregation had no clear end, until she reached out for Jesus.

Read the following text. Imagine you are the woman. When you reach out toward Jesus, are you afraid?

Text

Matthew 9: [20] *Then suddenly a woman who had been suffering from hemorrhages for twelve years came up behind (Jesus) and touched the fringe of his cloak,* [21] *for she said to herself, "If I only touch his cloak, I will be made well."*

[22] *Jesus turned, and seeing her he said, "Take heart, daughter; your faith has made you well." And instantly the woman was made well.*

Concept in the Text

As with other characters in the gospel narratives, we don't know this woman's name. And, in the spirit of this book, we will treat her as a person; she is not just an illness. As Kierkegaard said, *When you label me, you negate me.* To avoid negating her with a label like "the woman with the flow of blood," I am going to call her Amy because 'Amy' means 'Loved.' Amy must have had a strong sense of self for her to move toward Jesus in the way that she does. If she was unaware of being loved and valued at the beginning of the story, she is certain by the end.

Amy has three problems that we can identify in the passage.

Amy has a physical problem. Her physical problem is a continuous hemorrhage of blood which she had suffered from for a dozen years. Though most women experienced this as part of their regular cycle, she has it constantly. The consequences are several, one of which was weakness due to the loss of blood.

Amy has a social problem. The religious leaders of the day, the social norm and even the Holy Scriptures declared her 'unclean' because of her continuous flow of blood. The scriptures were clear. The Leviticus 15 law was well known, *25 If a woman has a discharge of blood for many days... all the days of the discharge she shall continue in uncleanness; as in the days of her impurity, she shall be unclean. 26 Every bed on which she lies during all the days of her discharge shall be treated as the bed of her impurity; and everything on which she sits shall be unclean 27... And whoever touches these things shall be unclean, and shall wash his clothes, and bathe himself in water, and be unclean until the evening.* Society, especially religious society, considered her soiled, contaminated, dirty, and unclean.

Finally, Amy has a personal problem. As other unclean people, she had been segregated, assigned distance, placed on the outside. This is her personal problem, as far as we know, up until this moment in the text, she has accepted her place on the outside.

Then Amy moves from her isolation toward Jesus. In spite of her physical weakness, in spite of her social separation, she pushes through the crowd toward Jesus. She reaches out to him in spite of her isolation as unclean. And in spite of her separation as a woman (women don't reach out and touch a man who is not their husband). In reaching out, she is made well.

Concept in Depth

Being ostracized is far too common today and far more than a game. In the beginning of her book, *Queen Bees and Wannabes,* Rosalind Wiseman describes this incident (a common occurrence) at middle school...

Mrs. Clarke, a well meaning but clueless fifth-grade PE teacher, tells the girls to get into a circle for a game. Mrs. Clarke wonders why it takes the girls so long to get into a simple circle. The reason, which she fails to see, is right in front of her. Who will hold hands with whom? As the girls vie for the various positions that will display their social status of the day, Mrs. Clarke gets impatient and yells at the girls to get it together – now! And then a horrible thing happens. Carla, the most popular girl in the grade, happens to be standing next to Cynthia to hold her hand? As their hands touch, Carla grazes Cynthia's fingers and then jumps away as if she's touched a dead fish. The other girls giggle...[xviii]

In groups today, as in Jesus' day, there are insiders and outsiders, popular and unpopular, clean and unclean, cootie-free and cootified. In all of these dualistic divided groups, to have them both, to have insiders and outsiders, it takes an agreement on both parties. For example, in the game of cooties, you can't have people with cooties unless those designated as cootified agree that they have cooties and that cooties are bad. If they neither agree they have cooties, or proclaim that having cooties is wonderful, there is no game. In a similar manner, you can't have people who are unclean unless they agree that they are unclean and that being unclean is bad. It takes an agreement on both parties for the dualistic arrangement to work.

Let me put it in a more personal context. When I was in early high school, I was clearly a 'nerd' and Peggy was 'cool'. (Sad to say, our language was still affected by the show *Happy Days* as we let Richie and Fonzie shape how we defined 'insiders and outsiders.') Peggy hung out with older guys with cars, most of them athletes. Peggy and I saw little of each other at school, but the summer after sophomore year, we spent a week together on a church trip. We grew close. At the end of the week, I said to Peggy, "I'd like to see you when we get back." I didn't know what it meant, I just said it.

"I'd like that," she said. And then she said, "Call me."

'Call me?' I had never imagined I would call her – or that she would want me to. What would I say? What would I call her for? To go out...on a date? I wanted to go out with Peggy, but calling her? The wide gap between cool and nerd, between girls who dated older guys with cars and me seemed insurmountable. Did I call her? No. Why? She terrified me. Not she, nor culture, nor 'cool' kids or 'nerd' set my distance from her on their own. I chose it. I didn't call her because the very idea made my hands sweat and my mouth mute. I agreed to the distance between us. Together, insiders and outsiders, we agreed to the separation. Again, for any segregation to exist, you need the segregators and segregates to agree on placement. You can't have 'cool' kids and 'nerds' in the same way unless the 'nerds' agree that being a 'nerd' is bad. Who knew?

In the text, as far as we know, Amy had been defined by culture, scripture and those in power as an outsider, as less than – and she had accepted it – until this moment. Here, she moves. She comes out of the dark. She doesn't stay back. She approaches Jesus. She crosses the distance others had set for her and she had accepted. She refuses the placement of any leader and any scripture that would call her 'less than.' She reaches and touches Jesus and in doing so is made well. And, likely, if history shows us anything, she gave permission to other women to do the same.

Application

In 1943, Rosa Parks got on board a bus in Montgomery. If you were black in Montgomery in 1943, you got on the front door of the bus, paid your fare, and then had to exit the bus and reenter by the back door which was the accepted entrance for blacks. But in 1943, a tired Rosa Parks entered the bus, paid her fare but instead of exiting to reenter just walked down the aisle and took her seat. The bus driver was James Blake, a young man recently back from World War II. Blake refused to drive the bus. He told her that she would have to exit the bus and reenter at the appropriate door in the back. After Rosa exited, Blake refused to open the rear doors and then drove off and left her. He was trying to teach her a lesson. She had to walk home.

Twelve years later, the same bus driver, though Rosa didn't realize it at the time, was driving when she got on board after working at a department store. She paid her fare and sat in an empty seat in the first row of back seats reserved for blacks in the "colored" section. As the bus traveled along its regular route, all of the white-only seats in the bus filled up. Bus drivers, if the white section filled up, were supposed to reassign seats for the whites.

Blake noted that the front of the bus was filled with white

134

passengers and that there were two or three white men standing. He then moved the "colored" section sign behind Rosa and demanded that she and three others give up their seats in the middle section so that the white passengers could sit down. Parks would later recall, "When that white driver stepped back toward us, when he waved his hand and ordered us up and out of our seats, I felt a determination cover my body like a quilt on a winter night. When he saw me still sitting, he asked if I was going to stand up, and I said, 'No, I'm not.' And he said, 'Well, if you don't stand up, I'm going to have to call the police and have you arrested.' I said, 'You may do that.'"

In her biography, *My Story,* she would later write, "People always say that I didn't give up my seat because I was tired, but that isn't true. I was not tired physically, or no more tired than I usually was at the end of a working day. I was not old, although some people have an image of me as being old then. I was   forty-two. No, the only tired I was, was tired of giving in."

Like Amy in the text, Rosa refused her placement. She wasn't going to play by the bus rules, the rules of the city, or the U.S. government. People could do what they want, arrest her, throw her in jail, but she was not going to take a seat as 'less than.' Was the bus driver an evil man? No. Were the police evil? No. Did Rosa Parks want to destroy them? No. She just refused to be placed as 'less than.' She refused to be treated, in her own words, as a "second class citizen." Through refusing her assignment as an outsider, she showed others we never have to accept placement as 'less than.' We never have to accept where others assign us. We always have a choice. We can always move (or not move in Rosa Parks' case).

Yet, how do we know what's right? Did Amy know how right her movement was when she started toward Jesus? Did Rosa Parks know how right her movement was when she remained in her seat?

The litmus test from this text and the story of Rosa Parks is simple. Right movement makes us well. Jesus tells Amy after she reaches out to him that "Her faith made her well." Right movement makes us well. If I move toward my family, my neighbors, my coworkers in a way that makes me ill, there is something wrong with the movement. Right movement makes us well.

Right movement also liberates others to move. Following Rosa Park's bravery, others realized that it takes two groups to play at insiders and outsiders. Others realized that they, too, had a choice. Others were liberated. Likely, when Amy reached out to Jesus, others were liberated to do so as well.

Challenge for Us

We can always move. No one can designate us as outsiders, and as insiders we can reach out to whomever we choose. Dividing lines are arbitrary. Jesus challenges us to cross and recross all arbitrary separations. It only takes one to change the world for others.

Reflection

Read the following quotes. How do they apply to the concept and stories above?

Deceive yourself no longer that you are helpless in the face of what is done to you. Acknowledge but that you have been mistaken, and all effects of your mistakes will disappear. – Helen Schuman

Each man must have his I; it is more necessary to him than bread; and if he does not find scope for it within the existing institutions he will be likely to make trouble.– Charles Horton Cooley

I think it's unfair, but they have the right as fallible, screwed-up humans to be unfair; that's the human condition. -- Albert Ellis

Acceptance is not love. You love a person because he or she has lovable traits, but you accept everybody just because they're alive and human. – Albert Ellis

Exercise

Think back to labels you have been given by others. Did a location of distance go with the label? Did you accept it or reject it?

How have you given labels to others that assigned distance? Is there a way you can move toward them now?

Flock of Sheep
Camille Pissarro 1888

*There can be no vulnerability without risk;
there can be no community without vulnerability;
there can be no peace, and ultimately no life,
without community.*
– M. Scott Peck

Chapter Twelve: Sheep and Goats

Primary Concept:
Our best measure of mental health
is how well we connect and relate to others.

Imagine a banquet table with the best food you have ever seen spread out in front of you. Around you are lots of people, but they, like you are starving. They look around the table, eyes longing, faces pale, countenance drooping. In your hand is a six foot long fork. You cannot let go of it. You cannot eat without it. No matter how hard you try, no matter how much food you get on the fork, you cannot bring any to your mouth. The fork is too long so you go hungry. This is hell.

Imagine the same banquet table, the same forks, but the faces around you are different. People are happy, faces rosy, voices chipper. No one is hungry. Others, like you are using their forks to feed others across the table. You feed and are fed. This is heaven.

Read the following story of Jesus. How do the sheep illustrate the image of heaven above and the goats illustrate the image of hell?

Text

Matthew 25:*31 "When the Son of Man comes in his glory, and all the angels with him, then he will sit on the throne of his glory. 32 All the nations will be gathered before him, and he will separate people one from another as a shepherd separates the sheep from the goats, 33 and he will put the sheep at his right hand and the goats at the left.*

34 Then the king will say to those at his right hand, 'Come, you that are blessed by my Father, inherit the kingdom prepared for you from the foundation of the world; 35 for I was hungry and you gave me food, I was thirsty and you gave me something to drink, I was a stranger and you welcomed me, 36 I was naked and you gave me clothing, I was sick and you took care of me, I was in prison and you visited me.'

37 Then the righteous will answer him, 'Lord, when was it that we saw you hungry and gave you food, or thirsty and gave you something to drink? ³⁸ *And when was it that we saw you a stranger and welcomed you, or naked and gave you clothing?* ³⁹ *And when was it that we saw you sick or in prison and visited you?'*

⁴⁰ *And the king will answer them, 'Truly I tell you, just as you did it to one of the least of these who are members of my family, you did it to me.'*

⁴¹ *Then he will say to those at his left hand, 'You that are accursed, depart from me into the eternal fire prepared for the devil and his angels;* ⁴² *for I was hungry and you gave me no food, I was thirsty and you gave me nothing to drink,* ⁴³ *I was a stranger and you did not welcome me, naked and you did not give me clothing, sick and in prison and you did not visit me.'*

⁴⁴ *Then they also will answer, 'Lord, when was it that we saw you hungry or thirsty or a stranger or naked or sick or in prison, and did not take care of you?'* ⁴⁵ *Then he will answer them, 'Truly I tell you, just as you did not do it to one of the least of these, you did not do it to me.'* ⁴⁶ *And these will go away into eternal punishment, but the righteous into eternal life."*

Concept in the Text

Two thousand years after Jesus lived; people are still debating his identity. Ironically, Jesus in the gospels is far more concerned with what we believe about others than what we think about him. Certainly, in the parable above, what the sheep and goats do separates them, but in their speech, and in the Son of Man's speech to them, their attitudes shine through. Likely their thinking is at the heart of their actions.

When they hear the judgment placed upon them, both goats and sheep alike are surprised. Their surprise reveals their perspective — specifically, their perspective about those in need. What Jesus says to the goats, how they heard it, and their response is best illustrated with a little highlighting. The Son of Man says to them, ***I** was hungry and you gave **me** no food, **I** was thirsty and you gave **me** nothing to drink,* ⁴³ ***I** was a stranger and you did not welcome **me**, naked and you did not give **me** clothing, sick and in prison and you did not visit **me**.'* ⁴⁴ *Then they also will answer, 'Lord, when was it that we saw **you** hungry or thirsty or a stranger or naked* *or sick or in prison, and did not take care of **you**?'* *45 Then he will answer them, 'Truly I tell you, just as you did not do it to one of the least of these, you did not do it to **me**.'*

The goats did not feed, clothe, or essentially help any of those described. They complain at the unfairness of the judge's accusation. The response is, "That's not fair! We didn't know that the hungry, thirsty, strange, naked, sick, imprisoned person we saw was **you**. If we had known it was **you** we would have done something!" They don't understand and in their protest show their bias. They only perceived that they hadn't helped the judge, not that they hadn't helped people in need. "Nobody told us it was **you**. If someone would have told us, we would have helped **you**. **You** would have been worthy of our help." The goats suffered from a dualistic mindset. For the goats, there was **us** (goats) and **them** (not goats). Others are clearly not us, clearly less than, clearly other.

Now, the sheep were just as surprised as the goats at the words of the judge. The sheep, through their surprise, also exhibit their attitude toward others. Again, with emphasis for understanding, the Son of Man says to them, *I was hungry and you gave **me** food, I was thirsty and you gave **me** something to drink, I was a stranger and you welcomed **me**, 36 I was naked and you gave **me** clothing, I was sick and you took care of **me**, I was in prison and you visited **me**.'* In their surprise, they respond, *'Lord, when was it that we saw **you** hungry and gave **you** food, or thirsty and gave **you** something to drink? 38 And when was it that we saw **you** a stranger and welcomed **you**, or naked and gave **you** clothing? 39 And when was it that we saw **you** sick or in prison and visited **you**?' 40 And the king will answer them, 'Truly I tell you, just as you did it to one of the least of these who are members of my family, you did it to **me**.'*

The sheep acted. The sheep helped others. Their action was also, like the goats, rooted in their perspective. Sheep have a different mindset from goats in the parable. Whereas the goats perceived the hungry, the thirsty, the stranger, the naked, the sick or the prisoner as other, as **them**, the sheep didn't. The sheep saw no others, no less than, no them, just us. The difference wasn't in value but need. Whereas the goats had a dualistic mindset of **us** and **them**, for the sheep, there was simply **us**. Surely there were people in need and people who weren't, but there was no distinction of in and out. Jesus hints at this difference between the two groups in their judgment. To the sheep, the Son of Man calls the *least of these who are members of my family,* and for the goats, they are simply referred to as *the least of these* without the family marker. Make no mistake, the sheep aren't doing charity by helping those in need, they are simply helping out other members of their "family." They did not see any distinction. Just **us**.

Concept in Depth

For Alfred Adler, the clearest indicator of a person's mental health was social interest. For Adler, we are all social beings. We all want to belong and find our place in the group. All our problems are, to some degree, social problems and involve our relating with others. Our ability to cooperate instead of compete is a sign of our mental health.

This social interest, this sense of **us** instead of **us** and **them**, is a sign of health of not just individuals but groups, including communities. In Martha's Vineyard in the early 1700's, was a great example of the sheep from Jesus' parable. On the Vineyard, due to the isolation of the community and the intermarrying, about one in ten people were born without the ability to hear. Later, in the twentieth century, mobility increased and the anomaly disappeared. During this time, deafness wasn't an individual problem, it was a communal problem. Everyone in the community, hearing and non hearing alike, spoke a unique sign language.

Historian Nora Groce studied the community and compared the experience of the hearing people to non hearing people. She found that 80% of the non hearing people graduated from high school as did 80% of the hearing people. She found that 90% of the non hearing people got married compared to about 92% of the hearing. They had about equal number of children. Their income levels were similar as were the variety and distribution of their occupations.

She then did a comparative study with the deaf on the Massachusetts mainland. At the time Massachusetts was considered to have the best services in the nation for the deaf. In her study, she found that 50% of the non hearing people graduated from high school compared to 75% of the hearing. Non hearing people married half the time while hearing people married 90% of the time. She found that 40% of the non hearing people had children while 80% of the hearing people did. Non hearing people received about one third of the income of the hearing people, and their range of occupations was much more limited.

Groce wondered how on an island with no services that non hearing people were as much like hearing people as could be measured, but thirty miles away, with the most advanced services available, non hearing people lived lives so lacking in quality from their hearing neighbors. How was it, Groce wondered, that on an island with no services, non hearing people were as much like hearing people as you could possibly measure. Yet 30 miles away, with the most advanced services available, non hearing people lived much poorer lives than the hearing.[xix]

The answer is simple, there were sheep living on the island and goats occupying the mainland. On the mainland, the deaf had a problem. On the island, the community had a hearing problem. On the mainland, they gave charity. On the island, they lived in solidarity. On the mainland, there were dualities of us and them, on the island, there was just us.

Application

Let me tell you about my friend Rodney. Rodney is also a minister. I am a part of a denomination that dates back 400 years to its start with John Calvin. He is part of a denomination (with one church) that dates back sixteen years to its start with him at a Bible study he taught while working for Saturn Automotive Corp. Our church is almost two hundred years old and has been at one location. His church is sixteen years old and is currently at its fourth location. I am a Presbyterian. He is a *Nondenominational, spirit filled, charismatic, evangelical, modern day, bapticostal, you want some of this here? kind of church.*

At their church, when the congregation wants to affirm something you said in a sermon, they yell, "Amen!" or "That's right!" At our church when they want to affirm something you said in a sermon, if you are paying close attention, you might notice a subtle nod. At our church, we look warily on a hymn that isn't at least fifty years old. At their church, they often sing songs they wrote on Saturday for Sunday's service. At their church, they use their hands as part of worship clapping and waving them. At our church members use their hands to check off items on the order of worship in the bulletin. At our church, if I said, "God told me to tell you..." I would be considered a blasphemer and expect some sort of stoning in the parking lot. At their church, if he said, "God told me to tell you..." he would be considered as doing his job and expect a second offering. At their church, their symbol for God is wind which blows through and brings change. At our church, our symbol for God is rock. God gives stability.

Through our relationship, I, and my congregation, have been challenged on our love for stability. Certainly a by product of faith can be stability and security, but, like any other good thing, we can love them too much. At our church, we talked once about moving our location and a few people left the church (even though the church didn't move). At their church, they talk about moving and more people join. At their church, they hope for change and want God to change the world. At our church, we talk about how bad it is that things change and, when pushed, will admit that the thought of God changing the world makes us nervous. (Perhaps that's why our services are so time limited – an hour and out – why risk something more?)

Because their congregation values change in a way we are learning to, they are much more open to risk. I have seen too often in our denomination, when thinking about a new church, we look for growth corridors, new subdivisions, and income. In Rodney's church, when choosing their last location, they looked for need. Their last choice of location was an area of Nashville not noted for the growth of subdivisions but for the increase of crime. We love our church's mission, but are challenged by theirs. At their church, they have this as part of their mission statement, *To be a community church, to finally bridge the gap between all races, rival denominations and churches, while becoming a catalyst for the unification of the Body of Christ.* At our church we are learning from their example as we are challenged to broaden our mission to include bridging gaps between races, denominations, and uniting churches.

Presbyterians and *nondenominational, spirit filled, charismatic, evangelical, modern day, bapticostal, you want some of this here?* kinds of churches can work together. Unified mission begins with unified vision, seeing not us and them, but simply us. That's who we are. And all God's people say, "Baaaaaaaaa."

Challenge for Us

The psychology of Jesus sees others as part of the whole. We are all connected, part of a larger **us.** For Alfred Adler, this was mental health. For Jesus, this was spiritual health. For all of us, this is our hope. The challenge is to take the perspective of the sheep, the perspective Jesus encourages, seeing only us. If we do, who knows? Heaven may abound.

Reflection

When you judge another, you do not define them, you define yourself. – Wayne Dyer

In the final analysis, says the Christian ethic, every man must be respected because God loves him. The worth of an individual does not lie in the measure of his intellect, his racial origin, or his social position. Human worth lies in relatedness to God. An individual has value because he has value to God. Whenever this is recognized, "whiteness" and "blackness" pass away as determinants in a relationship and "son" and "brother" are substituted. – Martin Luther King

Your task is not to seek for love, but merely to seek and find all the barriers within yourself that you have built against it. – Helen Schucman

The point in history at which we stand is full of promise and danger. The world will either move forward toward unity and widely shared prosperity – or it will move apart. – Franklin D. Roosevelt

Exercise

What groups of people have you defined has **them**?

What individuals have you defined as **them**?

How can you move toward them? How can you find solidarity with them? How can they become an **us** for you?

Who do you need to move closer toward to have a healthier, fuller, and more sheep like, life?

What will you do?

About the Author

David Jones is a Pastor
and author of the following books:

The Psychology of Jesus:
Practical Help for Living in Relationship

Jesus Zens You
(Formerly published as
The Enlightenment of Jesus:
Practical Steps to Life Awake)

Enough!
And Other Magic Words to Transform Your Life

Moses and Mickey Mouse:
How to Find Holy Ground in the
Magic Kingdom and Other
Unusual Places

For the Love of Sophia
Wisdom Stories from Around the World
And Across the Ages

Prayer Primer

Going Nuts! (Fiction)

For more information on these books,
go to: www.davidjonespub.com

Bibliography
Suggested Reading

Adler, Alfred; *What Life Could Mean to You – Alfred Adler on the Psychology of Personal Development;* Oneworld Publications; 1998.

Claypool, John; *Stories Jesus Still Tells;* Cowley Publications; 2000. Glasser, William; *Choice Theory: A New Psychology of Personal Freedom;* Harper Collins; 1998.

Faber, Adele and Elaine Mazlish; *How to Talk So Kids Will Listen & Listen So Kids Will Talk*; Scribner; 2012

Kohn, Alphie; *Unconditional Parenting;* Atria; 2006.

Nouwen, Henri; *Life of the Beloved;* The Crossroad Publishing Company; 1996.

Rosenberg, Marshall; *Nonviolent Communication – A Language of Life;* Puddledancer Press; 2003.

Wubbolding, Robert; *Using Reality Therapy;* Harper Paperbacks; 1988.

Yacconelli, Mike; *Messy Spirituality;* Zondervan; 2007.

For Counselors and further reading...

Adler, Alfred; *Understanding Human Nature;* Greenberg; 1946.

Connell, Gary, Tammy Mitten and William Bumberry; *Reshaping Family Relationships: The Symbolic Therapy of Carl Whitaker;* Taylor and Francis; 1999. Glasser, William; *Reality Therapy – A New Approach to Psychiatry*; Harper Row; 1965.

Glasser, William; *Warning: Psychiatry Can Be Hazardous to Your Mental Health;* Harper Paperbacks; 2004.

McCann, Eileen *The Two-Step, The Dance Toward Intimacy*; Grove Press; 1994.

Leahy, Robert L.; *Cognitive Therapy Techniques – A Practitioner's Guide;* The Guilford Press; 2003.

Walen, Susan R., Raymond DiGiuseppe and Richard L. Wessler; *A Practitioners Guide to Rational-Emotive Therapy;* Oxford University Press; 1980.

Wubbolding, Robert; *Reality Therapy for the 21 st Century;* George H. Buchanan Co.; 2002.

Also Referenced

Augsburger, David W.; *Conflict Mediation Across Cultures: Pathways and Patterns;* Westminster/John Knox Press; 1992.

Becker, Ernest; *The Denial of Death;* The Free Press; 1973.

Cone, James; *God of the Oppressed*; Seabury Press; 1975.

Corey, Gerald; *Theory and Practice of Counseling and Psychotherapy, Sixth Edition;* Wadsworth Publishing; 2000.

Dreikurs, Rudolf; *The Challenge of Marriage*; Hawthorne Books; 1946. Fritz, Robert; *The Path of Least Resistance;* Ballantine Books; 1989. Fulghum, Robert; *All I Really Need to Know I Learned in Kindergarten*; Villard Books; 1988.

Greeley, Andrew M.; *Star Bright*; Tom Doherty Associates; 1997.

Kubler-Ross, Elisabeth; *On Life After Death;* Celestial Arts; 1991.

Kurtz, Ernest and Katherine Ketcham; *The Spirituality of Imperfection: Storytelling and the Search for Meaning;* Bantam; 1993.

Peck, Scott; *Further Along the Road Less Traveled;* Simon and Schuster; 1993. Phillips, Robert; *Spinach Days;* John Hopkins; 2003.

Thompson, Rosemary; *Counseling Techniques: Improving Relationships with Others, Ourselves, Our Families, and Our Environment;* Psychology Press, 2003. Wink, Walter; *Engaging the Powers*; Augsburg Fortress; 1992.

Wiseman, Rosalind; *Queen Bees and Wannabes*; Piatkus Books; 2003.

Bible: Unless otherwise noted, the Bible version used was The New Revised Standard.

Endnotes

[i] *Online Etymology Dictionary*. Douglas Harper, Historian. 19 Mar. 2008.

[ii] *How to Talk So Kids Will Listen & Listen So Kids Will Talk*, Adele Faber and Elaine Mazlish, Scribner, 2012.

[iii] Mike Yacconelli, *Messy Spirituality*.

[iv] This idea of two types of love originated for me from a sermon by John Claypool.

[v] Elisabeth Kubler-Ross, *On Life After Death*, p.63-64.

[vi] Scott Peck, *Further Along the Road Less Traveled*, p.210.

[vii] Henri Nouwen, *Life of the Beloved*, p.61.

[viii] Thanks to Erik Masanger of Adler University for his help on Adler history and theory.

[ix] Summarized from Robert Wubbolding, *Using Reality Therapy*, pp. 28-57.

[x] Adapted from *Theory and Practice of Counseling and Psychotherapy* (6th Edition) by Gerald Corey.

[xi] Robert L. Leahy, *Cognitive Therapy Techniques,* p. 12.

[xii] William Glasser, *Choice Theory: A New Psychology of Personal Freedom,* p.5.

[xiii] William Glasser, *Choice Theory: A New Psychology of Personal Freedom*, pp.3-24.

[xiv] Alphie Kohn, *Unconditional Parenting,* p.4.

[xv] William Glasser, *Choice Theory: A New Psychology of Personal Freedom*, pp.3-24.

[xvi] David W. Augsburger, *Conflict Mediation Across Cultures: Pathways and Patterns,* pp. 286-7.

[xvii] Rosemary Thompson, *Counseling Techniques: Improving Relationships with Others, Ourselves, Our Families, and Our Environment;* pp. 76-77.

[xviii] Rosalind Wiseman, *Queen Bees and Wannabes*, p. 18.

[xix] 1991 PHEWA Newsletter.

Made in the USA
Charleston, SC
11 January 2017